Connecting with Ourselves & Others as We Age

How to Remain Engaged over Your Life Span

AGING WITH FINESSE, BOOK 2

Mary L. Flett, PhD

Five Pillars of Aging Press

Sonoma, California

MARY L. FLETT, PHD

Published in the United States by:

Five Pillars of Aging Press	Five Pillars of Aging Press
P.O. Box 134	157 Temelec Circle
El Verano, CA 95433	Sonoma, CA 95476

https://fivepillarsofaging.com
Five Pillars of Aging Press First Edition, 2021
First Printing
Cover Design: Jessica Reed

Book Layout © 2017 BookDesignTemplates.com
Connecting with Ourselves and Others as We Age. -- 1st ed.
ISBN: 978-1-7342395-6-0

This book is dedicated to my mother,

Virginia Sipp Flett,

who found joy in connecting with others

and brought joy to all who knew her.

The fact is that relationships are the alchemy of life. They turn the dross of dailiness into gold. They make human community real. They provide what we need and wait in turn for us to give back.

—*Joan Chittister*

Contents

MARY L. FLETT, PHD

Preface

I STARTED WRITING A WEEKLY BLOG in November, 2017 for the Center for Aging and Values. This was my opportunity to explore issues that have essential importance to me as an aging adult and, at that time, to my patients. Since then, I have published a blog every Sunday including several guest blogs and a couple of reprints of blogs I thought had "legs".

In 2020, faced with the consequences of COVID, I decided to pull my blogs together and publish them in book format. This journey has resulted in the Aging with Finesse series, of which this is the second book. Contents differ slightly from the original postings (and are much improved) due of the excellent editorial eye of Cathy Cambron.

The writing here reflects four years of thoughts centered on how to stay engaged with aging. This is a broad topic, as it includes the physical, cognitive, emotional, spiritual, and psychological. All are aspects of what it means to be human, and all undergo changes as we age. Understanding the process in order to help others has been the focus of my professional life. Writing a weekly blog for the Center for Aging and Values has given me discipline and joy in exploring what these themes mean to me.

In my thirty-plus years of working with aging adults, I have heard and shared amazing stories. These have given me insights that apply to my own life choices. I hope that you will find them instructive, inspiring, and touching, too.

I have organized these writings around certain central themes, but there truly is no "right" or "wrong" way of reading. Feel free to open to any page and just dip in. Each shows the original date of publication, but are not organized chronologically.

Earlier ones may come across as prescriptive, but it is not my intention to tell you what you need to do. Rather, I hope you will use the information in the spirit I wrote it – sharing things I have learned that help me avoid pitfalls or at least be aware of the territory I am covering.

Later blogs speak more from the heart. These demonstrate both my growth as a writer over time and my letting go of the need to be the expert. After all, we are all experts in our own lives.

SEEKING
CONNECTION

Originally published May 26, 2019

This was written before COVID-19 forced us to become disconnected. I am pleased that what I wrote then remains sound.

WE ARE LIVING IN DISTRESSING TIMES. It is getting harder and harder to deny the accumulation of real and perceived threats that demand that we take some action. The nightly news is filled with hyperbole and facts related to catastrophic changes in the political and environmental landscape. The local news follows the "if it bleeds, it leads" rule, broken only by incongruous weather and sports stories. Tweets and postings on Instagram and Facebook cause the snowballing of memes and threads that both trigger and amplify our inner "fight-flight-or-freeze" response.

Where do we turn? How can we manage the increased levels of adrenaline coursing through our bodies? Historically we have looked to religious leaders and cultural institutions to address the moral and civic issues that impact our lives. How different this all feels in 2019!

A lasting refuge when I have felt isolated or disconnected is my family. For many of us, family represents unquestioned acceptance and support. Inevitably, as I grow older, those who used to embrace me when I was younger are no longer here. Elders from whom I once received counsel and reassurance now need me to provide these things to them. These changes leave me in limbo.

Disconnection

One theme that shows up in my practice and my private life is the disconnection many of us are feeling. I realize that several factors contribute to this feeling. Geographically, I have no family close by. While I have lived in California for more than half of my life, my roots go back to the Midwest. This is where most of my cousins still live. The older relatives have died, so the annual visits back there have stopped. We used to come together during the summer months and for holidays and celebrations, but these occasions now accommodate the younger generation, and I rarely attend any family gathering.

I have no children or grandchildren who need my help or advice or who are available to support and assist me with tasks, chores, or transportation needs. My husband's children are all grown and have grandchildren of their own. Their lives are contained within their very tight circle and rightly focused on the newest additions to the family tree.

I am a widow, which makes socializing challenging, since most folks I know are coupled. I go to movies with friends and dine out, but I miss the comfort and contentment of coming home to a partner.

I still work, which limits my availability for socializing, traveling, and volunteering. Work also consumes my attention and requires focus to keep the multiple plates spinning, since I am a sole practitioner and don't have staff. While these are my challenges, many of my clients as well as colleagues and friends can add to this list their physical challenges, aches and pains, transportation issues, and financial limitations.

Consequences of Disconnection

It is easy to understand why so many older Americans feel isolated or cut off. It should not come as a surprise that this kind of disconnection often leads to feeling keyed up or tense; feeling unusually restless; having difficulty concentrating because of worry; living with a fear that something awful may happen; experiencing feelings of loss of control, changes in appetite, or changes in sleeping patterns (more or less); experiencing anxiety; being indecisive; and feeling unworthy, guilty, or hopelessness. This list reflects symptoms of what is called "anxious distress" and "depression." At some level, all these symptoms taken together or in combination can be readily identified in myself or others.

I am constantly amazed at how, in spite of the intensity and frequency of these symptoms, so many of us just keep on getting up in the morning and living our lives. Perhaps even more frightening is that we are coming to accept that this is just how life is.

According to the World Health Organization, depression is the leading cause of disability in the world. Read that sentence again, please. In. The. World. I want to let you know that it doesn't have to be this way!

Depression is an illness that has a beginning, a middle, and an end. Depression can be successfully treated with therapy and, if necessary, medication. We can live our lives with less anxious distress. Beyond the clinical approach, and perhaps within reach of us all, there is an essential intervention that can be applied. It is based on a bio-psycho-physiological truth.

We need each other.

The Antidote

The antidote to isolation and loneliness is connection. It is effective, however, only when we reach out to others. It can be accomplished in many ways. It can be done using social media, but it is ever so much more satisfying if it is done in person.

One of the most influential things my mother did in raising me was to take me with her after church on Sunday when she went to visit members of our church who were homebound. This was always a special time for me. We would bring flowers left over from decorations in the sanctuary, arrive at the person's home, and sit with them and just talk. I am not sure how long these visits were exactly, but they mustn't have lasted very long, since I don't remember being restless or wanting to hurry up and leave. I do remember the smiles and expressions of gratitude for this simplest of gestures, which for many represented the only human contact they had all week.

The Habit of Connecting

We lose the habit of reaching out to others when experiences of community-building are limited or change. Where once I was a part of several communities (work, school, church, and social), now I find myself resistant to joining in and protective of my time alone. I often succumb to feeling tired and depleted after a day of work. It is easier for me to click "Like" on a Facebook post than to actually pick up the phone and call someone.

Still, I am one of the lucky ones. I can drive at night, I have some disposable income, and I live in an area that is safe and offers a variety of events that restore me. While it takes more effort for me to participate in activities, even enjoyable ones, all that is required is my reaching out. I recognize this fact and have made a commitment to say yes to opportunities so that I can reconnect, so that I can affirmatively support my own well-being through giving and receiving.

I encourage you to look for opportunities to connect or reconnect. There are widening gaps in our social webs. We need to strengthen these, as the days ahead appear to contain challenges we have not faced in several generations. This effort may need to start with one person, but it can grow exponentially when we are connected. Check out this inspirational video that proves my point.

LONELINESS IN THE AGE OF CONNECTEDNESS

Originally published March 11, 2018

THE GERONTOLOGICAL SOCIETY OF AMERICA recently published a report on the lack of social connectedness (Robert B. Hudson, "Lack of Social Connectedness and Its Consequences," *Public Policy & Aging Report* 27, no. 4 [January 13, 2018]: 121–123). This comprehensive report looks at an issue that is present in every culture but is rarely addressed by policy. How can we, as a society, establish norms for dealing with an existential state of being?

From a policy perspective, loneliness is a public health issue. According to the AARP Foundation, costs associated with loneliness include higher blood pressure (with its increased risk of stroke), decreased immunologic response to infections and flu, greater risk of heart disease, and earlier onset of dementia.

Treating the isolated older adult is challenging. Outcomes frequently reflect the gaps in service. Older patients often evidence poor adherence to treatment because they cannot fill prescriptions, make it to appointments, or understand the mass of paperwork required to protect their privacy. Services are limited because of a lack of community health providers who make home visits and skilled nursing beds for rehabilitation. Wait times in the emergency room at local hospitals continue to be problematic, since the ER serves many who are unable to access health care elsewhere.

The Human Cost

While it is very useful to look at loneliness from the perspective of public policy, it does not address the issue at its most human level. The intersection of scientific, social, and spiritual connectedness is an essential one to understand. There is the psychological experience of separateness that contributes to and may be at the root of anxiety. There is the social experience of disconnection from family and community arising from technology and lack of opportunity to engage in social activities, and there is the spiritual experience of "I and Thou" and facing mortality.

From the vantage point of a philosopher, there is no end of writings that address this topic. Poets, too, explore what it means to be alone. What the report brings into focus is that there is an increasing social cost not to just the individual but also to our communities. Different groups of people must learn to connect in order to survive!

Cohort Isolation

It is not news that older Americans as a group are becoming increasingly isolated. For many years studies have identified infrastructure issues (such as lack of transportation), economics (threats to social safety net programs including Social Security, the Supplemental Nutrition Assistance Program, and Medicare), ageism, and technology as contributors to this phenomenon. Each of these has different costs and implications but, when taken together, result in a diminished sense of community and a profound loss of connection for aging adults.

Infrastructure issues affect all Americans but especially those who depend on public transportation. If people are unable to get to grocery stores, pharmacies, medical offices, and places of worship, their quality of life diminishes. This difficulty is particularly a problem for people in rural communities, where services are geographically spread out and public transportation is infrequent and limited.

The economics of aging is especially challenging here in the United States, because unlike other countries, the two most expensive costs associated with growing old (health care and housing) are unregulated and currently under siege by some elected officials at both the federal and state levels. In many instances, these economic disparities are only partly addressed by local government or charity and suffer from the vagaries of fundraising and allocation of competing resources.

Invisibility of Aging

Older adults become "invisible" in our culture as they age. Many live in self-segregated communities that contribute to diminishing opportunities for meaningful interactions with younger people. For older adults on the wealthier end of the economic spectrum, this looks like a retirement community. For those on the poorer end, this looks like Section 8 housing in a transitioning neighborhood affected by racism and economic decline.

Media have a profound impact on the perception of what it means to be old, and media portrayals continue to reinforce aversion to the aging process. Older adults are often portrayed as stupid or slow, having little familiarity with technology, and needing assistance to complete the most basic of tasks. Only occasionally are they shown as wisdom givers or respected elders who are consulted when difficulties arise.

Ironically, technology holds the greatest promise in "reconnecting" isolated older adults. It is not without its challenges, however. For example, barriers must be overcome, such as the cost and availability of Wi-Fi; issues of privacy; endless upgrades of software; problems of interoperability; and, for some, a learning curve in using smartphones, laptops, or whatever the next-generation device is.

What Should Be Changed?

Recommendations for change are found at many different levels. Essential research is being done by academic institutions and think tanks. AARP is but one organization that is publishing findings. What remains is finding the will to fund pilot programs and put into practice solutions that will make a difference. This needs to be done at the community level, with leadership from elders within each community. We need to step up to the plate and take the reins.

Some of us are living in communities that are proactively addressing and meeting the needs of the aging adults who live there. Others of us, as the AARP report highlights, are cut off from the essential element that preserves our humanity—connection with others.

The Center for Aging & Values has a ten-point matrix outlining what we believe it takes to create an "Elder-Friendly Community." The key elements are housing, health care, nutrition, transportation, employment, recreation, spiritual needs, creative expression, opportunities for lifelong learning, and intergenerational sharing.

There is no doubt in my mind that elder-friendly communities benefit from the wisdom and experience older adults can provide. Tapping this resource, however, is often a disorganized and reactive experiment rather than a planned initiative. Opportunities for exchange of information, sharing of mutual interests, collaborating, and problem-solving are antidotes to loneliness and feelings of disconnection. We need to create more of these.

BECOMING A PATHFINDER

Originally published September 30, 2018

I WAS IN GIRL SCOUTS growing up. One of the badges I spent time on was my Pathfinder badge. As I remember, I had to accomplish a series of tasks that demonstrated I could think my way through a problem, work with others on a project, and light a fire in the woods to keep myself safe and warm. In acquiring this badge, I had the benefit of regular interactions with older Girl Scouts and troop leaders, having a guide and instructions to follow, and the reward at the end of the project—my coveted badge.

I wish aging were more like earning a Girl Scouts badge. As we age, we are faced with a series of tasks. These include learning to adapt and accommodate to the changes in our functioning, adjusting to different kinds of loss, and expanding our collaboration with others on solving problems with finances, housing, health, and companionship. Other tasks involve coming to terms with our mortality and finding purpose and meaning in our lives even when what we think and do is no longer valued. Some of us will be more successful with this process than others. Some of us may not complete all the tasks.

Requirements of Aging

What is required of me is that I stay engaged in all the domains of my life. Staying physically engaged requires that I exercise and make good choices in what I eat. Staying cognitively engaged means trying new things and doing old things in a different way. Staying socially engaged encourages me to have meals with friends, go to movies, and check Facebook. Staying spiritually engaged asks me to go within as well as heeding my desire to give back and create a legacy of meaning for those who follow.

Necessary Skills

I have many mentors who have taught me skills. The legacy I inherited from my grandfather sustains me to this day. He was stalwart in his faith, tolerant and patient, and grateful for everything he had. That model of faith, tolerance, and compassion was not unique to him, but because I loved him and he loved me, it became imprinted in my psyche. I have developed a skill set and knowledge base that serve me in decreasing my fears about aging. I have a sense of peace as I enter into my young old age because I have watched family, friends, and patients successfully navigate their elderhood even in the face of Alzheimer's disease, chronic pain, and loneliness.

It has been my privilege to know exceptional elders who lived to their late eighties and nineties and who continued to be present and active in engaging with their lives. They provided me with templates showing me what can be ignored and what I must pay attention to. Their approach includes ignoring minor aches and pains and not taking things personally. Paying attention to being grateful and expressing love daily are essential.

Tasks that continue to challenge me include facing my mortality. I remain relatively healthy. Many of my peers are alive. But I have lost my grandparents, my parents, and my husband. So I am perhaps more adept with grief and loneliness than some of my peers.

I continue to find purpose and meaning in exploring aging through my writing and work with elders. I am beginning to expand my circle of friends and acquire new partners in addressing the needs of all people in my community, regardless of age. I am joining with others who are already working on projects and plans for creating safe places for people to age and recruiting others to care for us as we do.

Perhaps the most important task of a pathfinder is to know how to make our way through uncharted territory and take that information back with us, so those who follow can make their way more easily.

Training Manual

We are exploring new territory that, while familiar in some ways, carries with it unique challenges such as adapting technology to meet the needs of those of us who are not technologically inclined. Guidelines are needed to help younger generations connect with us. We recognize the increased speed of change but prefer to stay firmly anchored in the past. Our guidebook for exploring this territory is a bit thin and definitely outdated.

We need to find ways to stay connected emotionally and psychologically when disease or distance are barriers. We need to find ways to keep people in our communities instead of hiding them away in nursing homes or "golden ghettos." Updated guidelines are needed for managing behaviors that cause others distress but are not responsive to medication or instruction because the brain no longer has the capacity to change.

Addressing Change

We are exploring new territory in a time fraught with instability and threat. Planning for evacuation of a few older people in the face of fire, flood, earthquake, or other disaster once meant obtaining enough wheelchairs and a bus. Now, planning for disasters involves moving whole communities to new locations, perhaps never to return. There is little infrastructure in place to handle even occasional disasters. Better planning is needed to address this problem on a regular basis.

We need collaboration at all levels of government to identify and prioritize funding sources to ensure that elders receive the care they need instead of being abandoned. Building capacity for the total number of aging adults who will be unable to care for themselves is challenging. It is made more so because once the boomers have died off, all that capacity will no longer be needed.

We need to light the fire of compassion and create systems of care that will keep all of us safe and warm. We must come to terms with our collective denial of aging. We can learn, as I have, to appreciate the wisdom and insight that comes from having lived through times like these before. We need to seek and make use of this collective wisdom instead of diminishing its value and assuming incompetence.

Responsibilities and Rewards

As pathfinders, it is our responsibility to create a legacy of values for those who follow—to collect and curate the best of what went before and make sure this information is shared and available to those who come after. We must take a stand against being marginalized and make our voices heard, not in strident tones of righteousness, but out of a collective sense of purpose to preserve what is best.

What is our reward? I don't know what the badge would look like. I suspect it might contain a weathered face, with fine lines around the eyes from laughing a lot and having had a good cry or two. The hair (if there were hair at all) would be gray, denoting the passage of time. There would be a twinkle in the eyes that comes from recalling happy times and loving memories. There would be hands, perhaps with joints slightly bent or swollen, that demonstrate a masterful and tender touch. And there would be a heart, with evidence of breaks, but still beating strong. This is a badge worth acquiring.

DON'T CALL ME "MISS"

Originally published April 7, 2019

I WAS AT THE GROCERY store this week. Standing in the checkout line I listened to the exchanges between the customer in front of me and the checkout person. He was "youthful." In all likelihood, this was among his first jobs. He was busily scanning the items, looking at the computer screen, and attempting what appeared to be a well-rehearsed soliloquy.

The standardized patter went something like this: "Hello, Miss. Did you find everything you wanted? . . . Do you want to purchase a bag or did you bring your own? . . . . . Do you want to donate to charity? . . . Do you want your receipt?" It would appear that the rush of questions did not actually require any antiphonal response on my part.

Mind you, this was a soliloquy, not an actual conversation. Several things were missing that would help to structure and define this as an actual exchange between two people. For example, there was no eye contact. When he offered a greeting, he did not pause for a response.

This script prompted several lines of inquiry for me. If I hadn't found everything I needed, why would I wait until I was in the checkout line to let someone know? I would deduce that having placed my cloth bag on the checkout counter, the need to purchase another one would seem to be obviated.

Can You Hear Me Now?

I have stood in many a line where the checkout person swiped my items and carried on a conversation with the person in line behind me. Or with a fellow employee. Or totally stopped doing what they were doing and entered into a conversation with another coworker. Why? Was it because I was old? Was it because I am a woman? Was it because I am short or wear glasses or have a "do not disturb" look about me?

But what really gets to me is being called "Miss." Of all the possible salutations, I am completely befuddled as to how this young person determined that I should be called "Miss." I grew up in an era where I was taught to address those older than myself by using the terms "Sir" and "Ma'am." This young man had been directed to call me "Miss." I asked him, rather pointedly, why he did that? After figuring out that I actually wanted to have a conversation with him, he said it was store policy. This is a confusing policy to me, since it does not seem respectful or accurate.

Social Etiquette

I actually pay attention to proper titles. Having achieved high academic qualification, as well as a nationally recognized professional license, I take a great deal of pride in being correctly addressed as "Doctor." Now, this poor young man would have no idea about my professional standing, but he was able to discern that I was not a peer. He could have scanned my hands for jewelry and found that I am wearing a ring on my left hand, fourth finger. That is a culturally accepted symbol of being married. That would have dictated my being addressed at least as "Mrs." or "Ma'am." Yet there was a store policy to call older women "Miss."

Why? Is this some coy attempt at flattery? Is it designed to cultivate my custom so that I will return again and again to purchase goods from this fine establishment? I have my doubts. I actually made the young man pause, and after his embarrassment at not having an answer, I took him off the hook and said, "I am not a 'Miss.' There is nothing amiss with me! Please call me 'Ma'am.'" He didn't get it.

Crusty Old Fogey

Not to sound too much like a crusty old fogey, I have noticed an overall decline in manners. Perhaps this is more geographical. Perhaps more formal means of address are to be found where there is greater attention paid to tradition. Here in California, we are more informal. Still, I find myself noticing how much I could do with a bit more formality.

For example, I was in my office the other day. I work with three other therapists. Two of us are PhDs and the other two have master's degrees. One of the master's degree holders was in with her daughter, who was in her early teens. The therapist introduced me to her daughter by my first name: "Sally, this is Mary." Not "Sally, this is

Dr. Flett." Or Sally, this is Dr. Mary." Nope. "Sally, this is Mary." The introduction struck me as way too informal. While I appreciate that titles can actually get in the way of relationships, there is benefit to acknowledging both age and academic achievement in certain situations. This was one of them.

Channeling Maya Angelou

In a synchronistic way, my feelings on this exchange were brought home to me when I recently viewed an old clip of Maya Angelou speaking to a young, black woman on a San Francisco talk show, *People Are Talking*. I could not find the original of that clip, but you can Google it.

When I watched this clip, I said *"Amen!"* and then I wished I could channel Dr. Angelou. I realized that while others may call me by various names, most younger people are not taught the importance of honoring their elders through language. This is not about ego or status. It is about respect.

It may not come as a surprise to you that I strongly feel that elders in the United States are not treated with the respect we deserve. Maybe this lack of respect has come from a lowering of standards or because we are not wanting to identify with being "old." It may have its origin in our anti-establishment ways of the 1960s. Breaking down class barriers actually has some merit! But not in this instance.

Dr. Angelou said it brilliantly in her teaching moment: "I'm not 'Maya.' I'm 62 years old. I have lived so long and tried so hard that a young woman like you, or any other, you have no license to come up to me and call me by my first name. That's first. Also, because at the same time, I am your mother, I am your auntie, I'm your teacher, I'm your professor. You see?"

Worthy of Respect

I have heard it said that respect is earned not given. But what does that mean? Dr. Angelou suggests that a life that has been lived, with all the effort it takes to arrive at 60 or 70 or 80 or 90 or 100 or beyond, should be a sufficient demonstration and worthy of respect.

When people are forced to do anything, the resulting action is f done out of compliance rather than choice. I would hope that as an elder I would not force others to respect me. Rather, I hope that by modeling the virtues, values, and behaviors that are worthy of respect, I would be worthy of respect. In respecting myself, respect from others would naturally follow.

Now when people ask me how I prefer to be addressed, I will say with humor, "I prefer Your Royal Highness, but that title has not yet been given to me. You may call me Dr. Flett."

A NEW NAME FOR OLD AGE

Originally published February 17, 2019

I HAVE BEEN THINKING A lot about what to call myself as I grow older. I really don't like being a "senior," silver or otherwise. I have been a "senior" twice already, once when I was in my early teens and once when I was in my early twenties. Both these "senior" periods were characterized by completion of specific curricula designed to launch me into adulthood. Having successfully graduated from both high school and college, I really don't want to have to undergo yet another "senior" year.

I also don't like "older adult." I have written about this term before. It seems to be a convenient add-on rather than a good descriptor of what this time of life really is. You may remember that developmental psychology identifies specific categories of old: "young old," "old," "older old," and "oldest old." Seems to me this meme has about run its course—the only place to go after "oldest old" is "really, really old."

Truth of the matter is, knowing what to call myself as I chug along chronologically is both helpful and a hindrance. It is helpful because it can quickly sort out things and allow my brain to focus on what is useful. It is a hindrance because that same sorting mechanism tends to categorize variables in broad swathes that end up creating negative stereotypes.

This brings up one of the most insidious problems of all. Not knowing what to call ourselves results in being absorbed into a void: *them.* It is easier to ignore "them" than to pay attention to "me."

The Dilemma of Naming

More and more writers, thinkers, journalists, and researchers are looking at this issue. It took social psychologists to identify the early developmental stages: infanthood, early childhood, childhood, teenager, and adulthood. The scientists based much of their work on identifying tasks associated with these stages.

The famous observer of childhood Jean Piaget noted the essential shift in a child's ability to separate herself from others, a significant phase in brain development. Social psychologist Erik Erikson designated specific tasks that needed to be addressed in terms of acquiring social skills over the life span, noting that not everyone achieves success, even though they are chronologically aging. Gerontologists built on these theoretical structures and explored what it means to grown older, thereby contributing to the notion that tasks and stages may extend beyond puberty and work life.

Now advertisers have us in their grasp. Twenty- and thirty-somethings are naming us, framing us, and locking us into categories of sales targets. You are all well aware of these marketing pitches this activity. There are more ads for medications for chronic diseases of old age (such as heart problems, arthritis, and diabetes), incontinence, erectile dysfunction, personal safety and security ("Help! I've fallen and I can't get up!"). We are depicted as energetic but with gray hair, smiling as we walk, garden, or engage in happy group gatherings.

Aaron Riney Advertising

These slices of life, though they may work well for advertisers, do not come close to exploring the variability within the baby boomer generation. It is that variability that makes naming us so challenging.

My proposal is that we call this time of our lives "elderhood." Just as we transitioned from childhood to adulthood, elderhood can encompass a broad range of ages, functioning, capacities, and tasks. To adopt Erik Erikson's model, tasks in elderhood might include transitioning from "doing" to "being" (for example, going from working to retiring), adapting to changing roles (such as parenting and grandparenting), managing isolation and loneliness (including changes in status like being partnered and unpartnered as a result of death, separation, or dementia), and coming to terms with mortality.

Elderhood is not a target or goal; rather, it is a phase that may encompass many years chronologically or may consist of transformation of body, mind, and soul within a short period. Within these boundaries will be found individuals who are demonstrating skills at adapting to new circumstances, new ideas, and new ways of being.

There will also be those who are less skilled and find themselves preferring to preserve their rituals and habits acquired over a lifetime. There will be those filled with wisdom and compassion, and those who no longer know who they are or who have succumbed to bitterness.

While research may further define and clarify all the elements to be found in elderhood, it is up to those of us who are exploring these new frontiers to claim this territory for our own. So, I am claiming "elderhood" as my name for growing old. I would delight in hearing your thoughts and ideas!

Some Additional Observations

There are so many opportunities in this age of media to address the stereotypes that create false understandings and fear about aging. Stereotypes arise from experiences and then become templates. When you were born has a lot to do with which stereotype of aging you grew up with. Search on YouTube for, "Young vs. Old," and you can find a number of videos about sterotyping and aging. Then go to the Project Implicit site at Harvard University, where research is being done on implicit bias, and check out your own beliefs about aging (click on "AgeIAT").

IS RETIREMENT AN OPTION?

Originally published April 15, 2018

I AM SPENDING TIME WITH a financial planner, since I turn sixty-five this year. While my medical costs will be covered by Medicare, how I pay for the rest of my expenses is up for grabs. I am very, very grateful that I will have medical coverage. But I wish I had done a better job of figuring out how to keep a roof over my head, gas in the car, and a few extra bucks in the bank.

What I don't have is a pension. I did not succeed in putting aside money in a 401K, as much of my life I worked in settings that were either nonprofit or public-sector. Unfortunately, I did not spend enough years in my various government jobs to become vested, so I am left with a small monthly Social Security check and some savings. Definitely not enough to see me through my seventies and into my eighties in the style I would like.

Closing the Gap

Other aging Americans are even less fortunate. Many have to find work in order to survive. According to the Bureau of Labor Statistics, older Americans are "projected to have faster rates of labor force growth annually than any other age groups. Over the entire 2014–24 decade, the labor force growth rate of the 65- to 74-year-old age group is expected to be about 55 percent, and the labor force growth rate of the 75-and-older age group is expected to be about 86 percent, compared with a 5-percent increase for the labor force as a whole." (https://www.bls.gov/careeroutlook/2017/article/older-workers.htm) What does this information suggest? The growth rate reflects a need to work *because many older adults don't have enough money to live on.*

The number of elders at or below the poverty line is increasing. According to the Henry J. Kaiser Foundation, in 2016 half of all people on Medicare had incomes less than $26,200. Key findings in a report published in November 2018 suggest that elder women, persons of color, and those who have health issues experience increased poverty rates as they age.

Unfortunately, fewer and fewer services are being funded by government, and there is decreased funding of services in the private nonprofit sector to address these gaps. For many older Americans, minimum wage jobs are essential to be able to afford medications, food, and day-to-day living expenses.

The recent budget passed by Congress with its promised tax reform will affect aging adults in poverty particularly harshly. Funding for rental assistance, social safety net programs including Meals on Wheels, and transportation were cut or eliminated. Elders living in rural communities may be even harder hit, since funding for these programs is traditionally limited to begin with.

We Need a Shift

What needs to be done to address these issues? Much more than just allocating money. A fundamental shift in how Americans view aging adults is required. If we continue to see older Americans as "drains" on our economy who cost money because of "entitlement programs" such as Social Security and Medicare (which to be clear, are *not* entitlements), we are demonizing a source of wisdom and potential working capital. We are also breaking a promise made by Presidents Franklin Roosevelt and Lyndon Johnson to ensure that all Americans can count on there being a safety net to see them through their old age.

While not all older Americans want to work or have the physical stamina to work full-time, those who do want to continue working should be looked upon as valued assets in a growing economy. Since the trends are away from lifetime employment, hiring an older worker to do part-time or seasonal work makes good sense. Older workers bring with them skill sets and a work ethic that enhances most work environments. Companies who hire older workers report gains made in job satisfaction and in safety. Productivity actually increases on teams in which older workers and younger workers share tasks.

Reasons for not hiring older workers typically focus on them being inflexible, unable to take instructions from someone younger, and lacking in computer skills. Such arguments are based on stereotypes and projections rather than actual data. Challenging the stereotype of older Americans being computer illiterate needs to be undertaken on all levels, but most especially by older Americans!

The American Way!

For many aging Americans, having a job reflects both a strong work ethic and a financial necessity. Finding that place where you feel you are making a difference, contributing to your community, and bringing home some money for your efforts often is at the foundation of feeling good about yourself. Having a job makes you feel engaged with life.

It's not like there isn't work to be done in our communities. Students need teachers. People need housing. Gardens and public spaces need care. Cars need repairs. Customers need customer service. Buses and cabs need to pick up passengers. Crops need harvesting. Food needs processing. Deliveries need to be made. Dogs need to be walked. People need to be cared for.

Will older workers command the same salary as when they were in the workforce? Will they be in the same jobs? The answer is no. The trend is for part-time employment at a low hourly wage.

My Plan . . .

What's my plan? Win the lottery? Find me a millionaire to marry? No, I plan to work as long as I am able. I am lucky because I am a psychologist and have a private practice. I am, therefore, not subject to ageism by my employer. Of course, self-employment has its challenges, but so far, I am holding my own.

We all want to remain productive across the life span. Having a purpose to get up in the morning makes life more exciting. We just need to come together in a collective effort to make things better for all of us.

MAY IS STROKE MONTH

Originally published May 20, 2018

A FEW WEEKS AGO, I wrote a blog about Tip-of-the-Tongue phenomena. While this is a relatively benign hiccup in the brain, today I want to look at a more serious threat to staying engaged as we age. This threat is stroke. According to the Centers for Disease Control, stroke is the leading cause of long-term disability and reduces mobility in more than half of all stroke survivors sixty-five and older.

What is a stroke? It is a threat to the brain. Blood flow is cut off, and brain cells start to die. Consequently, depending on how bad the stroke is, a person can lose the ability to speak, muscle control, or the ability to walk; experience memory problems; or even die.

Kinds of Stroke

There are three different kinds of stroke: ischemic stroke, hemorrhagic stroke, and transient ischemic attacks (TIA). Ischemic stroke is caused by a blockage in the blood vessel. Like damming up a river, a buildup in pressure occurs, preventing the flow of blood and causing blood pressure to get very high. Cholesterol is the primary culprit here, building up over years and clogging the arteries. Hemorrhagic stroke occurs when a blood vessel in the brain bursts or weakens. This causes blood to seep into the brain, literally cutting off blood supply and creating pooling. While rarer than ischemic stroke, hemorrhagic stroke often results in death or serious functional impairment.

TIAs are like smoke alarms. They are indicators that you need to take some action, right away! Blood flow is temporarily stopped, signs of stroke appear, but somehow the blockage is resolved within twenty-four hours, and there are no apparent lasting effects. Pay attention, though! While the symptoms may go away, a TIA is an indicator that all is not well with the circulation to your brain.

Prevention Is the Best Strategy

Prevention is really the best strategy to manage the risk of stroke. Prevention is the reason your primary care provider encourages you to watch what you eat, take your statins as directed, exercise, and keep your blood sugar under control. Learning to manage stress is also important.

One of the reasons stroke can be so debilitating is that people often ignore the signs and symptoms and put off seeking emergency care. Knowing the signs of stroke and getting help immediately are essential for several reasons. First, if you are able to be treated quickly, the effects of the stroke may be reduced. Prompt treatment can result in full recovery for some people, or potentially better levels of functioning after rehabilitation if there isn't full recovery. Secondly, knowing the signs can help lower your anxiety when you are wondering whether forgetting a word means you are experiencing an emergency or just need more sleep.

So, what are the signs of stroke? The easily remembered acronym is *FAST*:

*F*ace drooping (one side of the face droops)

*A*rm weakness (when both arms are raised overhead, one drifts downward)

*S*peech difficulty (slurred speech, slow speech, inability to produce words at all)

*T*ime (This is an emergency! Time matters! Call 911 right away!)

This happened to my husband. He was sitting at our dining room table and I heard him mumble something. I asked him to repeat it and this time looked at him. His face was drooping and even though he thought he was making sense, the words coming out of his mouth were incomprehensible. I called 911 and we got him to the hospital.

The whole thing was very scary for both of us. I am happy to say that he recovered almost 100 percent through the help of a wonderful speech therapist and a change in his medications. He did have permanent changes, though, that included problems with handwriting and tiring more easily.

Speech and Stroke

Speech is one of the things that distinguish humans from other species. Language is one of the most complex tasks that our brain engages in. There are two aspects of language: producing it and understanding it. To understand what is being said to us, our brain uses about two-thirds of its energy to attend to the sound, make sense of the actual words, and place them in a context that can have multiple meanings.

Problems with the production of speech are called aphasias (from the Latin, meaning without language). To produce language, our brain relies on complex networks in different brain areas, specifically the motor cortex, Wernicke's area, and Broca's area. These networks send code that causes our tongue, mouth, throat, and diaphragm to coordinate to produce sound.

It Gets Complicated

The process of "naming" something requires that we hold a concept of the "thing" and then assign a label to it. "Doggy" and "Kitty" are labels we assign to dogs and cats. We further define these concepts through learning grammatical rules. "My doggy" is different from "the doggy," which isn't the same as "all doggies."

Remembering your pet's name for a password requires that you recall both the label and the grammar context (noun and tense) for the thing that belongs to you ("My doggy's name is Spot!").

Often stroke victims have difficulty in naming things and producing speech. This inability to successfully communicate adds to the experience of sadness and grief that frequently accompanies a stroke.

While aphasia is a sign of stroke, it can also occur in traumatic brain injury and in the later stages of many dementias (for example, Alzheimer's and frontotemporal dementia). Any loss of speech has a profound effect on the quality of life for the person who has lost his or her speech and for those who are providing care.

For a remarkably inspiring and informative introduction to what happens when the brain is experiencing a stroke, I encourage you to read *My Stroke of Insight: A Brain Scientist's Personal Journey* by Jill Bolte Taylor. If you don't have the inclination to read, you can listen to her TED Talk. Dr. Taylor's stroke happened when she was relatively young. Her recovery took ten years.

Sadly, many older Americans are unable to sustain the intense rehabilitation that is often needed to bring the brain "back online" after a stroke. Medicare covers only limited sessions with physical and occupational therapists. Many families have neither the money nor the commitment to continuing what is started in rehab, and so the stroke victim is left adapting to an increasing loss of functioning.

Preventing Stroke

An important takeaway from all this is to pay attention to changes in your overall ability to produce words. If you are just forgetting the name of a friend or a thing, make sure you get enough rest and cut yourself some slack while waiting for your brain to retrieve that word. If your face is drooping, you cannot raise your arms, and you aren't making sense with your words, then call 911! Exercise, keep your blood pressure under control, manage your blood sugar, and take medications as prescribed.

HELP! I NEED SOMEBODY!

Originally published June 9, 2019

THE BEATLE'S SONG "HELP" HAS been playing in my subconscious for weeks now. I first remember hearing the song, originally released in 1965, on *The Ed Sullivan Show*. One of my playmates in the neighborhood got the album (*Rubber Soul*), and we would play all those songs, over and over, memorizing the words and imitating the Fab Four. It never occurred to me that these lyrics would lay low all these years only to surface at this point in my life when their meaning has taken on new significance. (In case you have forgotten John Lennon's lyrics, you can find them online.)

I am needing more and more help these days because I have arthritis. I am temporarily using a cane until I can get hip replacement surgery. Canes are a universal sign of vulnerability. What I have noticed since using one is that many people will open doors for me. Many people offer to carry bags to my car, and kind souls will offer me a seat. I have also noticed that these acts of kindness seem to come from older adults.

My intention here is not to go into a rant about manners and how the youth of today don't seem to have any. It is more about John Lennon's observation that I do need help. I need to ask for it. And I need to express my appreciation.

Adapting to Change

Since I work exclusively with elders in my practice, I get to see a full range of functioning. For those with mobility issues like me, the focus of many of my sessions is on adapting to the changes needed to manage everyday life. These sessions include skill-building around pain management, as well as talking about medications, their side effects, and their interactions with other substances. I have purchased thick cushions for my chairs to make it easier for me to get up and down and have found several of my patients using them too.

Many of these conversations also reflect feelings of helplessness and exhaustion that are by-products of the effort needed to get in and out of bed, or into the shower, or in and out of the car. Well-meaning instructions to exercise more, stay optimistic, and remember what the goals are often fall on deaf ears—deaf not as a result of hearing loss, but of overwhelm.

Attitude Is Everything

What I have come to learn through my own experience as well as from my patients is that attitude is everything. Central to that attitude is being willing to ask for help, regardless of the outcome. Help will not always be provided, and it may not be provided in the way I want it. But that shouldn't stop me for asking for help.

My nature is to want to do everything myself. In some ways, this attitude reflects those childhood stages of development when I learned to tie my own shoes, drive a car, and take on responsibilities. I became capable because of my independence. I don't want anybody thinking that I can't do things or that I am weak or vulnerable. I want people to see me as strong and capable. I like being the person who helps other people!

Asking for Help

Because I no longer can perform at the levels I used to, I am now gaining experience in asking for help. Doing so is risky for me. My inner critic is having a field day giving me advice about how silly and stupid I am to have let my physical self get so compromised. There is also a chorus about how I should have planned better for getting somewhere on time. I drown these inner voices out by swearing every time it hurts. Of course, there is an alternative.

Asking for help is a risky strategy. There is the possibility that help may not be available. There is the possibility that help will be denied. There may be a negative history around asking for help in the past" maybe, for clarity that now has become a self-fulfilling prophecy that no one cares and no one is ever going to be there for me. There may be cultural and linguistic issues that interfere with being understood.

There may be internal scripts, replete with drill sergeants shouting insults intended to motivate but successful only in shaming. In my case, I concluded long ago that it was better just to keep quiet and do things myself. I confess I have had a difficult time challenging that assumption. But circumstances have forced me to change my ways.

Rewards for Asking

In making this change, I have found many rewards in asking for help. More often than not, the person I ask has the answers I am looking for. In some cases, the person becomes an advocate or ally who is available when I am feeling down. Many have provided unexpected and pleasant distractions to my habitual ways of engaging with the world.

When I put my inner critic on mute and just attend to my needs, I find more often than not that people are kind, helpful, and caring. There is empathy from those who have similar limitations and often shared solutions to problems or resources. There is camaraderie and knowing glances that frequently result in brief conversations with people I never would have chatted with. There is a feeling that I am not alone and evidence that I can get through this experience, reassured by the fact that others have successfully done so.

So thank you, John Lennon. Thanks for letting me know that I can ask for help.

A CALL TO ACTION
(IT'S NOT WHAT
YOU MAY THINK)

Originally published June 17, 2018

I HAVE BEEN FEELING QUITE disconnected this week. I have found myself distracted, impatient, and generally out of sorts. Some of this feeling is no doubt the result of my returning from a long weekend away, where my routine was pleasantly upended and disturbed by being in nature and experiencing a different environment.

Within my small circle of geographic touchpoints (gas station, store, pharmacy, coffee places), I have experienced new levels of awareness. For example, gas prices are at an all-time high in my area. Yet I put my credit card into the machine, fill up the car, and go on without the emotional charge of *"yikes!"* Seeing as I can remember gas wars from the 1960s, when gas was a mere 20 to 30 cents per gallon, you would think I would be jumping up and down at having to pay over $3.00! But, no, I just put the card in, take it out, and go on my way.

This is just one example of my disconnection from reality. I read and listened to news reports this week of children being separated from their parents, put in cages, and held at the border. All this on the orders of a man holding the position of highest ethics in the land: the attorney general of the United States. I was outraged! I was outraged in the quiet of my living room. I was outraged in front of my mobile phone feed. I was outraged at my desktop. I was outraged in my privileged solitary confinement.

Today, as I listened to news reports explaining what had occurred halfway around the world in Singapore, I felt what is now a familiar swelling of righteousness. A friend posted a question on her Facebook page asking why people weren't out in the streets protesting. After all, mine was the generation that marched on Washington to stop the Vietnam War, to right the wrongs of years of civil rights abuses and segregation, to ensure equal pay for equal work. Mine was the generation that created newsworthy protests!

Then I looked at myself in the mirror. While the outrage burns within, I am no longer connected in any visceral way to communities of action. I express my outrage through emojis. I discharge my discomfort with pithy posts. I find solace in reading what others say, especially those I agree with. I have limited bandwidth to stay engaged in discourse or discussion with someone who holds a differing opinion.

In taking stock of this state of things, I also see how my role as a leader in in my community has changed with age. I am now on the sidelines of power. I am dismissed not because of my beliefs, but because I have aged out. Without a Twitter following or hourly posts on Instagram, I have become a relic, posting on Facebook for the benefit of a small circle of "friends." A quaint caricature of an older person befuddled by technology and a step behind whatever is current.

What Is My Role?

We are living in an age that is demanding the return of moral leadership. What is my role as an aging American? I am spending time considering what this truly means.

Having experienced upheaval in the late 1960s and through the mid-1970s, I know the vulnerabilities of being a passive citizen. Our country is seeing the effects of Timothy Leary's instruction to "tune in, turn on, drop out." The evolution of the revolution is that we have eviscerated community and instead become separate and self-contained, not always individually, but in "only people like me" groups.

Developmental systems theory (Urie Bronfenbrenner) posits that we each exist within a context of spheres of influence starting with our family and expanding to the community at large. Within each of these spheres are values and beliefs that influence our behaviors. Where my generation has fallen short is in making sure those who follow us understand the need to stay in relationship with our inner circle and expanding spheres.

With the rise of the Internet, what had historically been geographically and time-based spheres (neighborhoods and distance) evolved into immediate and unlimited connection. It is my contention that the result has been a rewiring of our connections, in some cases creating disconnection.

Call to Action

Action is called for right now. Perhaps not the action of my youth—the burning of flags, the marching in the streets—but action nonetheless. The channels where action now manifests are markedly different from the 1960s. We must vote. We must share our values and beliefs with others not just online but in person, face-to-face, heart to heart.

High Tech/High Touch

While I was in graduate school, I had the privilege of working at SRI International. One of the scientists there presented on his work creating the Internet. The title of his talk was "High Tech/High Touch." His premise was simple. As wonderful as all the technology was, we absolutely needed to ensure that we remained connected at a human level and acted in humane ways.

There is a visceral lack of humanity present in the world right now. We are all witnesses to it because of our technology. Now we need to bring some heart to the table. This is the call to action that I am going to answer.

A PLAN FOR ACTION (NOT WHAT YOU THINK)

Originally published June 24, 2018

LAST WEEK I WROTE ABOUT my belief that as aging Americans we have to stretch beyond our comfort zones, connect with younger Americans, and share our wisdom if we are to address the imbalance in our society and government. I got lots of feedback on this post. One theme stood out—the question of how to take action.

The events that shaped my political awakening began with the election of John F. Kennedy and continued with the Civil Rights Movement and the war in Vietnam. I grew up in the suburbs of Chicago, originally from a Republican family in which my father's side had voted Republican even during Franklin Delano Roosevelt's terms in the White House. My mother's side of the family, because of a strong German and Irish Catholic heritage, broke ranks and voted Democratic when JFK ran. And you better believe that there was lots of fallout!

The late 1960s through 1975 were a time of incredible social upheaval in the United States. Many of us believed that the revolution was at hand. As a teenager, I marched to protest unfair housing practices. I marched on Washington to protest the war. I took action in my high school to address inequality and unfair representation. This was my political laboratory. I was inspired by older Americans and acted with the energy of youth.

I learned to make speeches, to talk with elected representatives, to write to newspapers, and make calls to talk shows. All of these venues were the state of the art back then and required little more than thinking through what I was going to say and making the effort to send a letter or postcard. Still, there was a learning curve. Truth is, I didn't know how to do these things until I felt passionate enough about what was going on to take action.

Oh, how things have changed!

Or have they? Perhaps things have speeded up with the Internet, but essentially the work is the same. Effort is needed to contact your elected representatives, call in to talk shows, and make speeches. Effort is also needed, more now than ever, to seek out and find sources of information that are reliable. All that is required is passion and willingness to act.

So here are fifty ways you can take action:

1. Call your elected representatives (local, state, and federal) and leave a message on their phone lines.
2. Email your elected representatives.
3. Send postcards to your elected representatives.
4. Visit the local offices of your elected officials and ask to speak with someone about your concerns.
5. Have a brief statement ready to read. Something like: "I am a constituent of Senator So-and-So. I am opposed to . . . (or I am in support of . . .). Please ensure that when you vote on that issue my position is taken into account."
6. Write a letter to your local newspaper.
7. Make a call to a local talk show.
8. Write an editorial and send it to your local PBS station (radio and TV).
9. Post a video on your Facebook account using your cell phone.

10. Host a consciousness-raising party. Invite people over to talk about their concerns and fears.
11. Start a petition.
12. Donate to an organization that is supportive of your beliefs, then tell your friends and family you donated.
13. Host a "Pol-Party" to which you invite people who are interested in learning more about how to run for office. Contact your local Democrat or Republican (or Socialist, Green, or other) Party for instructions.
14. Read a newspaper from another city where you don't live.
15. Share stories of your political awakenings with your family and friends.
16. Attend meetings at your city hall, county government, or state capital.
17. Offer to speak in a high-school history class about your experiences at an event you participated in (such as the March on Washington).
18. Write a letter to your grandchildren (or other young people) about why you believe in the future of this country.
19. Offer to drive people to their voting locations on Election Day.
20. Help people sign up to vote.

21. Support a candidate either by giving money or by volunteering.
22. Turn off your TV and talk with your neighbors.
23. Create a Meetup group for discussing local issues.
24. Believe that what you do matters, then go do it.
25. Practice expressing yourself until you feel confident, then speak up!
26. Practice saying, "I have a different point of view. Here's how I see us coming together."
27. Practice listening.
28. Practice having a conversation, not a shouting match.
29. Take time to identify what is scary for you. Take steps to address your fear(s) not by withdrawing, but by learning to soothe yourself.
30. Seek to understand before you offer suggestions or opinions: "Let me see if I understand what you are saying . . ."
31. Increase your capacity for being around things that make you uncomfortable. Start with the easy stuff—try a new food.
32. Speak your own truth, not a statement that has been given to you by someone else.
33. Assume that you are wrong every once in a while.
34. Find things you have in common with others instead of looking for ways you are different.

35. Consider that the changes you desire may be the very things someone else fears the most. Learn to address their fears and make them feel less threatened.

36. If you catch people when they are having a bad day, cut them some slack and try again.

37. Be persistent.

38. Be kind.

39. Get the facts *and* the feelings.

40. Reflect on all the ways you have changed in your lifetime and share these changes as hope for the future.

41. Do as much as you can, but not more than you can handle.

42. Bake cookies for Election Day.

43. Become a poll watcher.

44. If you haven't already, register to vote.

45. Identify how you came to your beliefs; be willing to question them.

46. Find ways to agree.

47. Meet your neighbors.

48. Hang out with people younger than you.

49. Read biographies of the founding fathers.

50. Vote!

Let's go change the world!

TRAVELS WITHOUT CHARLEY

Originally published April 28, 2019

I REMEMBER READING JOHN STEINBECK'S travelogue *Travels with Charley* when I was in my early teens. I couldn't put it down. That book opened my eyes to a world very different from my suburban life outside of Chicago. This past week I have been taking my own travels, but without Charley. I have driven from the West Coast, going south to the greater Los Angeles area, then across the open expanses of the Southwest, and I now am finally adapted to the altitude and climate of Santa Fe, New Mexico.

I have written before of the benefits of travel. The changes in routine, the different stimuli awaken and lay down new neurological pathways. The different sights, sounds, and (for me) tastes of local cuisine all create sparks in the brain that renew cognitive functioning. Those benefits aside, there is also the remarkable transformation of routine, shifting from autopilot in my daily existence at home to finding the rhythm of life on the road and a comfortable bed.

Modes of Transport

Over the years, I have traveled to different parts of New Mexico, Arizona, and California by car, train, and plane. I think my favorite way to travel is by train. I am forever amazed and inspired by the vision and doggedness of those who originally laid down tracks and crossed this country. I try not to romanticize this history, but I find myself setting aside what must have been terrible suffering and sacrifice and just visualizing what it must have been like for those who met in the middle of nowhere and drove the Golden Spike connecting the country. That moment of triumph and realization of the enormous potential of train travel.

My second preferred way of travel is by car. I come from a family of drivers. Back in the day when gas cost pennies a gallon, my grandmother used to take me for drives in the country in her 1948 Buick Roadmaster. These were adventures on back roads between Chicago and her hometown of Watertown, Wisconsin. There would be roadside stops to pick up flowers, buy sweet corn in the summer, pick wild asparagus from the roadside (not yet sprayed with chemicals) in the spring, and purchase margarine in Illinois before crossing the state line to Wisconsin, where margarine was not sold because, after all, Wisconsin was the Dairy State.

Ooohhs and Ahhhs

I told folks I was planning to drive to Santa Fe and got the most amazing collection of responses, ranging from "What a great trip!" to "Goodness! That is so far away! You're going to drive that way all by yourself?" It never occurred to me that driving that distance might be out of the ordinary or something that people would not consider doing. After all, I was a child who grew up benefiting from Eisenhower's vision of creating a National Highway System that would improve commerce and provide backup landing strips in times of war.

For me, the benefit of driving by myself is that I get uninterrupted time with my thoughts. I am skilled enough in mindfulness practice to actually crave such uninterrupted time. I find my thoughts have much more space between them when I am driving than when I am sitting and meditating. I find myself laughing out loud at the absurdity of some of those thoughts. Somehow, I don't notice them in the same way when they are scrunched together in my everyday life.

Is It Safe?

I do experience anxiety at times. I realize that as an older woman traveling alone, I might be seen as a target. I try to keep aware of my surroundings and not venture into areas that might subject me to harm. I like to think of myself as having good common sense as well as a sense of direction. My sense of direction has changed slightly, as I rely more and more on GPS and less on maps and getting a lay of the land.

This trip took me through parts of South Central LA where I had never been to because of rush hour traffic on the 210. Because I was relying on GPS, I had no idea where I was in terms of the neighborhood, but I was re-assured as I noticed that I was in a caravan of sorts with others like me who were following the same directions. We were like some oddly formed funeral procession.

Advantages

There are many advantages to driving. I can take more comforts of home with me than when I take a train or fly. I can decide when and where I want to stop. I am not a big fan of Yelp, instead relying on reports from friends and family who know the local haunts, what places to avoid, and where the best coffee is.

Once I get to my destination, I can drive around, get lost, and then find my way back to where I am staying. I do my best to stay away from chain restaurants but find them reassuring when I am new to an area.

Disadvantages

Of course, the downside to driving is the cost of gas these days. While there are countless apps that can direct me to the cheapest prices, in most states I still have to get out and pump it myself. The exception is Oregon, which is one of the most civilized states in the nation, in my humble opinion!

When I am on the road, I find long-buried loyalties to brands of gasoline I remember from my childhood. I suspect that the gas is actually pretty much the same, but I am still influenced by the symbols I know best. I also consider the brands I feel politically OK about purchasing and look for stations that are relatively close to the freeway.

Driving for hours across land interrupted only by distant mountains and clouds, I can easily imagine myself as a pioneer, walking no more than seven to ten miles a day, trusting that my guide would find us both water and a safe place to make camp. Crossing between Phoenix and Santa Fe, or driving from Denver to El Paso, the roads follow ancient trails laid down by the original inhabitants of this land.

I am in awe of Native Americans, who adapted to the harsh and unrelenting demands of finding potable water and creating sustainable agriculture in this land that is inexpressibly beautiful and without mercy. That these peoples did so and thrived is a testament to their hardiness and adaptability. That I am able to travel these distances in one day by car or in just hours by plane is a miracle.

In a few days I will be returning home. My route will be slightly different, but I will still partake of the hospitality of kind friends and family along the way. I will remember this trip for many reasons, in spite of having withstood the lure of taking pictures of my meals on my smartphone. Foremost among these is the gratitude I feel for living in such a remarkable country and having the privilege to take advantage of its many treasures and generosity of spirit.

COMINGS AND GOINGS

Originally published September 2, 2018

I AM ON VACATION THIS week and have been pondering how a change of environment impacts me. I noticed the anticipation of going somewhere is both exciting and mildly anxiety-provoking. Truth be told, I am a homebody and usually am content staying right where I am. My tendency when I do travel is to attempt to re-create my creature comforts as a strategy to soothe myself in strange places.

When I leave, I am focused on the arrival and have been told that I miss out on a lot of things because I am so intent on getting "there"—wherever "there" is. This preference is in stark contrast to the tendencies of my mother and my husband, who were both inveterate wanderers. Still, once I am "there," I am excited to go out and about and discover all kinds of new things.

My colleague and fellow blogger Mark Brady suggests that new environments are actually good for our brains. New stimuli spark neuronal growth. Our bodies adapt to new sounds, sights, and smells. Our digestive systems take in new foods, and our bacteria devour and transform them into useful energy. All of this activity is very exciting and, fortunately, goes on behind the scenes so that we don't have to put much conscious effort into it.

I remain in awe of the old-time explorers who were open to new experiences, had to adapt to whatever food was available, and didn't have a CVS or Safeway to make a quick stop to obtain a familiar and needed item. I know that I can find familiar foods in familiar restaurants and grocery stores whose names, menus, and layouts are just like what I can find at home. Having these options is both a good and bad thing. Predictability does lessen the chance that I will encounter a food or substance with which my body is unfamiliar, resulting in a possible negative gastrointestinal event. But turning to the predictable option also limits my exposure to new and untried things.

The experience of things being "different" can be anxiety-provoking. As a way of managing the anxiety, my unconscious brain will attempt to fit different faces and accents into tried-and-true patterns. This is a well-documented process that advertisers and marketers take advantage of.

For example, in a new location the weather is bound to be different, but the weather forecaster shares the information the same way. Ads on TV reflect local businesses with different names, but the sales pitch for new cars, mattresses, and "end-of-summer sales events" follows a familiar pattern. As I settle into a new experience, these things are reassuring to me, but oddly disappointing in their sameness.

Relaxation

Another benefit of getting away is relaxing. This benefit, too, comes from a change—a change in routine. So much of my work life is centered on timekeeping. When I am on vacation, I don't need to worry about being somewhere at an appointed time. My inner clock starts to take over, and I find a quieter and less insistent rhythm to my day.

In this quiet space, I find my thoughts coming and going. And unlike when I am in my regular routine, the spaces between those thoughts expand. This space is useful because there is so much clutter in my brain that I typically jump from thought to thought, from lily pad to lily pad, from memory to memory, and I often miss out on what is right in front of me. In this space, I can just rest on what is happening in the now.

Transitions

There have been many other comings and goings this month. People of note and influence whose lives ended: Aretha. John McCain. Neil Simon. People who lived large in the public eye. But others have also left us. August is particularly challenging for me, since so many of the people I loved and who loved me died in Augusts past. Life and death happen to all of us.

Yesterday, as I was driving, I noticed a spider being held to the windshield by the force of the air. As I slowed, the pressure eased, and the spider, no longer held in place, quickly crawled away. I don't know whether that spider was amazed or relieved or shocked. I don't know whether it returned to the ground or was swept away. But I do know its life was changed by forces out of its control as it was taken from an environment that was familiar and transported to somewhere the spider would never have gone under normal circumstances.

Watching this spider raised a variety of emotions in me, remembering how many times I had been transported to places that were new or different. Not always by my own choice. Requiring me to adapt to new things and incorporate the unfamiliar. Feeling unsure, vulnerable, scared, and even excited. And, when the pressure was lessened, finding myself again. Creating a new normal.

As I grow older, I am finding that comings and goings are actually a rhythm that is predictable but not constant. I sporadically pay more attention to this rhythm when my patterns change. Vacations offer an intentional change. Loss of a loved one so frequently results in unintended changes. My takeaway is to recognize how adaptable and flexible the human spirit is.

Return

I have a few days left before I return home. I suspect I will begin to transition into "going" mode shortly. Again, the anticipation of returning home will arise, but I am already changed by my being away. I will return with new eyes, new memories, and new commitments to ways of being.

I hope I will be able to stay true to these new commitments, since the benefits of a slower pace and taking time to care for my own needs are resulting in such positive changes. Doing so will require that I incorporate new patterns and new ways of paying attention. The familiar exerts its influence much like that force of air on the spider. Sometimes I cannot move because the familiar routines and habits hold me in place. It isn't until that pressure is eased that I find ways to escape or reposition myself.

I will view my home with changed eyes, perhaps now seeing what needs to be spruced up or changed or gotten rid of altogether. I will have new comparisons that will either reinforce my choices or make me see my environment more critically. Familiar faces will once again inform me of the local news, weather, and sports. And I will tune in or tune out the ads and return to that conversation in my head about how little there is for me to watch on TV.

But not for a few days yet.

BACK HOME

Originally published May 5, 2019

IN SOME WAYS EVERYTHING HAS changed and in others, nothing has. When I left two weeks ago, I remember feeling claustrophobic, short-tempered, and impatient. The thousand details that needed attention in order to pack everything I needed for my trip seemed to blur. I gave up trying to double-check the lists I made to ensure I didn't forget anything. I just surrendered to the intention, tossed things in the car, and headed south. Didn't even get twenty-five miles away and realized I had left maps, directions, and other documents back at home.

One of my areas for personal growth is overcoming a tendency toward stubbornness. Even though I was not twenty miles away from home and could have gone back for the papers, I watched my "monkey mind" work through the knotty problem of how I could re-create the information, what alternatives I had, and whether this

MARY L. FLETT, PHD

problem would be as cataclysmic as my now-triggered amygdala was insisting. My intervention was a venti nonfat decaf latte and a commitment to not look back.

Once under the hypnotic influence of interstate driving, I entered into a suspended state of animation, now at the direction of and totally supplicated to GPS driving instructions from a disembodied female voice telling me to watch out for vehicles on the side of the road and offering alternative routes available to bypass traffic. I pondered how easily I had given up authority and autonomy to this computer and followed, sheeplike, the instructions that took me into less than familiar places in areas I would normally avoid. The errant thought occasionally surfaced prodding me to question what would happen if I lost access to the GPS or my battery ran low.

In spite of these misgivings, I arrived safely at my first destination, embraced all the newness, adapted my nightly hygiene routine into a new order, and promptly fell asleep. This process would be repeated several times over my vacation, as I stopped to visit family and friends along the way and was received graciously at every venue.

Scouting Locations

While this vacation was designed to give me a well-earned rest, it was also an exploratory mission to check out possible sites to host Five Pillars of Aging five-day seminars. I have several criteria for these events. Seminar sites must be within an hour of a major airport; must be destinations that are able to accommodate a wide range of visitor activities, including upscale sleeping accommodations, sightseeing, catering, and convention services; and must be beautiful. This time I was looking specifically at Santa Fe, New Mexico. (By the way, it met all the criteria!)

The older I get, the more I rely on routine to keep me focused and not let things fall through the cracks. In this case, I needed to re-create my office, including computer, writing prompts, and work, as well as my health regimen. Since I was driving, I was able to pack my car with all the accoutrements of home: various containers holding laptops, files, plastic storage containers with pills, special foods, and perhaps most important my pillow. I must admit, I felt like a Victorian memsahib re-creating my slice of England in foreign lands, *sans* a retinue of servants.

I am amazed at how easily I adapted this template to the different places I stayed. From every venue I was able to access email, banking, and local and regional news, as well as stay up to speed with what was happening on Facebook and post my own updates. My amazement rises from my inner experience of disorientation, increased word-searching, and feeling just ever so slightly off balance.

Thinking this inner experience reflected on my cognitive decline and was a death knell for my ever being able to complete my dream, I paused and just related the same advice I give to my patients: "You are tired, and you just need to cut yourself some slack."

Novelty

All in all, I got to experience a multiplicity of wonderfully new (novel) experiences for my brain to grow new neural pathways. All of my senses were involved. New smells, new tastes (Christmas chili), new faces, new ideas, new music. My body adapted to different biomes, different levels of calcium in the water, and different foods. I experienced high desert, low desert, mountains, verdant valleys, dry washes and stream beds, and huge lakes in the middle of nowhere created by the damning of once mighty rivers.

And everywhere, people going about their lives and their routines, accommodating my life and its temporary and passing moments. Meeting new people (names forgotten, but stories remembered), reconnecting with beloved family and friends, recalling (or inventing) stories of a shared past, and committing to strengthening the bonds those memories rekindled are all ways and reasons that travel and visiting are essential to remaining engaged as we age.

In total, I traveled 2,859.4 miles. Slept at an elevation of 7,199 feet and drove through Death Valley at an elevation of 282 feet below sea level. My arrival home revealed a transformation of flowers and shrubs from budding to blooming. The intensity and ubiquity of the greens permeated my psyche now used to umbers and tans. I had left Sonoma just as spring was erupting and spent time in an area of our country that is stark in its chiaroscuro of adobe and clay against piercing blue skies and incomparably fluffy white clouds, but no less bursting with life.

Back Home

I'm doing errands today—reentering the rhythm of my life in Sonoma. The familiarity of these rituals brings a smile to my face and makes me appreciate the gifts of having my own life on my own terms. My life's potency has not yet succumbed to, which is simultaneously reassuring and habituating. In going away, I gained perspective on what is essential to me. What I cannot live without are good friends, good conversation, good food, and a good cup of coffee. The rest can be improvised.

FRIENDS AND VISITORS

Originally published June 2, 2019

I JUST SAID MY GOOD-BYES to one of my dearest friends, who came for a visit on her way to points south. We shared laughter, memories, food, and philosophy (and, truth be told, a glass or two of Prosecco). Having visitors is always delightful for me because it prompts me to look at how unconscious I have become in my "I live alone" routines.

In sharing my space, I get a chance to look at it through my friend's eyes. This perspective reawakens in me the memories accumulated through living in the same place for more than twenty years. What is merely background for me most of the time now comes into focus as visitors ask about artwork, or photographs, or the books on my shelves. My desire to make sure visitors feel comfortable highlights those nicks and knocks that I haven't repaired or touched up.

And then there are the directives echoing from my childhood telling me to get the house clean and ready and to put out the special towels for the guests. There is the newly awakened eye that sees the dust bunnies and clutter that normally I ignore. And there is the anticipation of arrival and heartwarming reunion when my visitors are here.

Conversations

What is most satisfying and truly satiating is having live, open-ended conversations. Living alone as I do, I find myself typically only exchanging pleasantries with store clerks, wait staff in restaurants, or other service folks. These conversations are brief, solution-focused, and rarely venture into personal philosophy. Conversation with friends typically takes place through texting or email. To be able to sit for hours across from a friend in my living room and share ideas, thoughts, debates, observations, insights, and confidences feels indulgent.

One of the joys of having lifelong friends is the accumulation of shared events, familiar stories, and intimacies that contribute to a certain easy flow and soothing pace of conversation. With newer friends, I find myself at times being cautious with what I am saying. I will self-edit until I feel more sure of how my messages will be received and let down some of my barriers in return.

With friends I have known for years, the conversations have a different pace, even though they may be covering familiar ground. Shared experiences from the past frequently veer off into stream-of-consciousness accountings of newer events. Sometimes there is an inclusive assumption that someone from my college years knows and loves a friend from another period of my life even though they have never met. The occasional furrowed brow is all that clues me in to the fact that I am the common thread, and these other folks don't know each other at all!

Stories shared multiple times are still enjoyed, even though the endings are known. Tolerance of these repetitions is easier with friends than with family members. "Have I told you this before?" is answered with "Yes, but tell me again!" instead of "Oh, please! Not that story again!"

Sharing

I do admit to needing to learn ways of sharing my space with others. I grew up in a Catholic neighborhood, and many of my childhood friends came from families of 6 or 8 or even 9. I remember going to friends' homes and seeing their shared rooms with bunk beds and shared closets. I was awestruck! As an only child, I had a room to myself and didn't have to share anything. I somehow was socialized successfully but still have a preference for having my own things instead of sharing.

I have a small home and have come to see it as my sanctuary. It is spacious enough for one but requires adaptations to include others. The irony is that for the majority of the time I have lived here, I shared it easily with my husband. And it seemed to magically expand when, at different times, two of his daughters and their children came to live with us.

In college I had roommates my first year but subsequently I found ways to have a room of my own. Like many young adults, I shared space in the first few apartments I lived in to save money. It wasn't until after more than twenty years of marriage and becoming a widow that I lived again on my own.

Now, I ponder what it would be like to have someone living with me and frankly have a hard time envisioning that possibility. This is why it is wonderful to have visitors: I get to practice sharing my space. I get to practice adapting to different schedules, preferences, and personalities.

Auntie Glad

I will always remember a conversation I had with my Auntie Glad. She wasn't actually my aunt; rather, she was a very close friend of our family. There was a family story that she had been sweet on my grandfather at one time, but I don't know that there was a whole lot of truth to that.

Auntie Glad had led a remarkable life for a woman coming from a small town in Wisconsin. She had graduated from Vassar in the 1920s, had enjoyed the social scene in New York, and became a social worker during the Depression. She eventually returned to that small town in Wisconsin and became a pillar of the community. She never married but lived alone in her family home surrounded by antiques and fine art. Our families stayed close throughout the decades, and my mother and I frequently visited with her in her older years.

We were having dinner one night. I was in my twenties and she was in her eighties. Sitting among the beautiful antiques and original artwork, and eating at a grand dining room table set with candles, fine china, crystal, and silver, I asked Auntie Glad what gave her a sense of pleasure and satisfaction. I was imagining she would answer by telling me stories of the good old days or talking about her life as a social worker. Instead, she looked me in the eye and said, "Friends."

I try to hold on to the preciousness of my friendships and the opportunities for staying in contact. There is a certain sweetness to the reunions and a bittersweetness to the leave-takings. The older I get, the more I appreciate that so many of these friendships were not coincidental or random. Each has provided a lesson or reinforced a belief that sustains me as I age. I have to agree with Auntie Glad.

ALL THE NEWS THAT'S FIT TO PRINT

Originally published January 13, 2019

I WAS RAISED IN AN ERA when the daily newspaper was a solid source of information, second only to the neighborhood gossip and Paul Harvey on radio. Newspapers came out with morning and afternoon editions and sometimes special editions. There were also weeklies and penny-savers. Newspapers were run by families of note who influenced opinion and politics.

I grew up in Chicago reading the *Chicago Tribune*, then owned by the McCormick family. The *New York Times* was owned by Ochs-Sulzberger family. The *Boston Globe* was run by the Taylor family; and we all know about Meryl Streep owning the *Washington Post*—sorry, I mean Katharine Graham. You could tell a person's politics by which paper he or she read, as well as which baseball team the person supported. And you could get all the baseball statistics you needed in the sports section.

Essentials

The essentials of life were covered within these pages, including births, deaths, marriages, and sales at local stores. Newspapers were read carefully. Information contained within was discussed among family, friends, and in classrooms all over the country. Opinions expressed were discussed at the dining room table, in bars, and at church socials.

There were competing papers in the big cities. Chicago had the *Tribune*, the *Daily News*, and the *Sun Times*. New York had the *Times*, the *Wall Street Journal*, the *Daily News*, and the *Post*. Boston had the *Globe*, the *Christian Science Monitor*, and the *Herald*. Washington, D.C., had the *Post*, the *Star*, and the *Daily News*.

The publishing industry was a major employer of all kinds of workers ranging from typesetters, paper boys (yes, boys!), distributors, and delivery truck drivers to reporters, editors, and printers. Apparently there was a lot of news to print!

Great Writers

And the writing was magnificent! I think of the great writers who either started or flourished in the land of the three-inch column: Ernest Hemingway, Studs Terkel, Mark Twain, Maya Angelou, Margaret Mitchell, and Charles Dickens, to name just a few. The gift these writers gave was to create word pictures of human experiences happening in real time. Whereas a picture might be worth a thousand words, the thousands of words these writers wrote continue to inspire long after we have scrolled through the picture books.

As a kid, first thing I would read in the *Chicago Daily News* was Mike Royko's column. When I lived in San Francisco, it was Herb Caen. Op-Ed pages in those days could sway voters, and endorsements were sought by politicians from all parties. People would vote based on the recommendations of the editors of the daily paper.

The Smell of Newsprint

There was a wonderful visceral relationship with the paper, ranging from the smooth, almost weightless touch of the paper to the smell of the newsprint and the sound of the rustling pages as they were turned. Once the information had been consumed, the paper itself continued to provide utility, as wrapping paper, package filler, liners for bird cages, or strips for papier-mâché projects. I remember newspapers holding French fries, steaming walnuts, and freshly fried donuts, as well as protecting carnations, roses, and bouquets of wildflowers.

I still read newspapers, but now I read them online. The experience isn't quite the same as actually holding a newspaper. The content remains important and useful, but the layout is different, and I miss the tactile engagement. I no longer have to lick my fingers to turn the pages and wash my hands after reading to get rid of the ink. I miss folding the paper, doing the crossword puzzle, and cutting out the cartoons.

Scanning the News

I also don't read the paper as carefully. My attention span is shorter. I am distracted by the visuals, the audio, and all the other tchotchkes that obscure the words on the screen. I click instead of lick, and turn the page using a mouse. It is not the same. Although I can post links to various social media platforms, doing so is not as satisfying as talking about the news with friends. And it certainly isn't the same as cutting out articles or clipping cartoons!

Still, I read newspapers every day. Now it is the *New York Times* and the *Washington Post*. My neighbor, who still gets her paper delivered, shares tidbits from the *Santa Rosa Press Democrat*. Even though there is now overt partisanship in the papers (as opposed to the covert partisanship that used to be there), I continue to rely on newspapers to bring me information that is dependable and useful in my daily life. And, I have to confess, just as my grandfather used to do, I read the obituaries first to make sure I'm not there.

Some Additional Thoughts

I grew up discussing current events in school and at home. These discussions did not resemble the talking heads shouting opinions at one another that have become a sport on cable news. These discussions were about knowing what was going on around the neighborhood and in the world so that we could participate as informed citizens. This still is a good model and a key component to staying engaged over the life span. Consider creating, joining, or encouraging others to engage in a current events group, using newspapers as source material. This is a great way to stay current, build community, and keep your mind active.

WHO WERE YOUR
ROLE MODELS?

Originally published January 27, 2019

WHO "TAUGHT" YOU HOW TO be old? The role models
I grew up with included my maternal grandfather (who
lived to eighty), my paternal grandmother (who lived into
her nineties), and cultural icons such as Grandma Moses
and the centenarians who made it to the *Today Show*'s
segment on folks turning one hundred with Willard
Scott (brought to you by Smuckers!).

My Grandfather

My grandfather's impact on me was enormous. I had
daily interactions with him throughout my life. These
evolved from being the sole grandchild, who was enter-
tained and adored, to becoming his caregiver after he
broke his hip in a fall and continuing to provide care as
he lost his ability to walk and became wheelchair-bound.

An active, vibrant man for the majority of his life, he easily and effortlessly climbed three flights of stairs to his flat daily and walked to and from work in downtown Chicago well into his early sixties. He broke his hip in a fall while entering his office building. Fortunately, my grandfather's fracture was successfully treated, his hip was surgically repaired, and he initially returned to almost fully functional status. Therein lies the rub.

Consequences

He did file a lawsuit for negligence on the part of the building owner. It took two years before my grandfather's case came to trial. During those years, his physical functioning declined and his world become smaller.

I have a vivid memory of being at the trial and watching him use his cane to navigate the space between the plaintiff's table and the witness stand. He rose with difficulty and walked slowly but with as much dignity as possible to take the stand, where he described what had happened and his subsequent decline in the ensuing two years. He won the case, but it was a Pyrrhic victory.

My grandfather was a widower. As he aged, his need for daily household help increased. Because he couldn't climb three flights of stairs any longer, my mother and I would visit him daily, do his shopping, bring him dinner, and make sure his laundry and the apartment were kept clean. I would stay during the weekends, both as a respite for my mother from me and as a respite for me from my mother.

Mentoring

These were remarkably wonderful experiences for me, as my grandfather was a very wise and compassionate man. I literally had twenty-four-hour access to him. It did not occur to me that, at ages fourteen to eighteen, I was too young to be providing intimate bathing and toileting care for an older man. Quite honestly, there were few options in those days, and it was expected in my family that we would do for each other. It was a practicum born of love, and I learned an awful lot about biological functions in an aging adult.

The biggest lesson for me was around giving and receiving. What my grandfather taught me is that while an individual's capacity to function may decline in his or her physical world, that person's spirit, mind, and personality can, and often do, remain strong.

Now I Am a Role Model

Ever since I celebrated my sixty-fifth birthday, I am keenly aware that I now have a very different idea of what sixty-five is from what I remember my idea of sixty-five being when I cared for my grandfather. I currently enjoy an active, unrestricted lifestyle. I expect to be working and feeling useful well into my seventies.

I have access to surgeons and insurance to cover the cost of hip replacement should my functioning decline and a reasonable expectation that this surgery will result in a return to full functioning within days. What is required of me is that I exercise, lose weight, and stay physically and socially engaged in activities that have purpose and meaning for me.

I have difficulty wrapping my mind around the number "sixty-five," since it does not reflect my inner experience of my energy, my thinking, or my short-term and long-term goals. I am not ready to step aside and "retire." Instead, I am planning and initiating what I call the "Last Third" of my life.

Adaptation

For me to do the things I intend to do and create the kind of life I want and expect, I will need to find ways to adapt to changing functional needs. I will need different strategies for preserving my independence and creating income streams. I will need different networks of friends and neighbors (since I don't have children of my own) to keep me connected and in touch with what is new and cutting-edge. I will need access to different medical specialties at different times. I will need connection and support in adapting to things that I cannot control. All of these needs require a mindset that is open and flexible.

I believe I have this mindset because I had a role model in my grandfather, who showed me how to adapt and accommodate to the unexpected challenges and surprising gifts that aging brings.

MISCELLANEOUS MEANDERINGS

Originally published March 10, 2019

PEOPLE OFTEN INQUIRE HOW I come up with ideas for this blog, and I wish I had a smart, snappy answer. Truth of the matter is, at this stage of my life, thoughts just seem to randomly enter my cognitive awareness. Some of them capture my attention. Some hold my attention. Some slip away, leaving a vaguely disturbing aftereffect suggesting I may have forgotten something important, like closing the garage door or turning off the oven.

Most of the time I am able to remain focused on my task (or at least give the impression that I am). Then there are the other times, when I find myself staring into the distance, suspended between the task and the daydream.

Judgment vs. Mindfulness

I once worked for a man who would sit at his desk, leaning back in a chair staring out the window. His arms would be crossed and his head cocked to one side. He could sit there, seemingly for hours, without moving. I, on the other hand, was working energetically with focused intensity, accomplishing mundane secretarial tasks. My judgmental (and admittedly jealous) mind castigated him for "just sitting there." I suspect he had little awareness of how I felt, nor would his behavior have changed if he had known he was being judged so harshly. He was content to look out his window.

Nowadays, I find myself staring out windows a lot. My need to be productive has undergone a transformation. I now give myself permission to slow down and enjoy some of the tasks I used to dash through. This change comes in part from my practice of mindfulness—a useful skill that serves me well and that keeps revealing new insights and nuances about my thoughts and behaviors.

Case in point: I found myself swearing out loud after a particularly frustrating experience getting out of a chair. I had sat too long, and my muscles and joints had given up sending me SOS messages about their need to move. When I once again became aware of my body and its needs, I attempted to respond and found the negotiations took longer than expected. My hips, knees, and assorted tendons were on strike and informed me through the use of sharp pain that immediate engagement was out of the question. I would need to move more mindfully and with intention, rather than just get up. After the scatological eruption finished, I found myself laughing and gently taking myself to task for not paying more attention to my body.

No Parking

Another example: I found myself circling the grocery store parking lot looking for a parking space that was optimal, given my current limitations in walking. For some reason, everybody in town had decided to show up at the grocery store at that very same moment and had procured all the parking spots I deemed optimal.

So I circled. As if I were in a landing pattern at JFK International Airport, I circled, and circled, and circled. It finally dawned on me that I could go elsewhere for what I wanted and could stop driving around in circles. But it took me several laps before I was able to disengage from my inner dialogue about how nobody would let an old lady in, how crowded this town was becoming, and how things were so much better in the good old days.

Communion

Last night I had dinner with two women friends. This was a spur-of-the moment dinner, and we all brought something. The food was nurturing, delicious, and shared with enthusiasm. The conversation was wide-ranging, covering politics, religion, Michael Jackson, racism, travel adventures, and recipes. There was an ease and flow that comes from genuine interest and enjoyment of each other's company. I came home feeling full.

As a single working woman, intimate gatherings are my preferred way to socialize. I notice these opportunities tend to be centered around meals. Sometimes the meal is brunch or dinner out, sometimes an impromptu evening in where an elegant table is set and new dishes are shared. I don't have a lot of stamina for late-night partying or hanging out at bars. I have no judgments about these activities—just not my cup of tea.

Weather

Today the rain is falling, and there are sheep in the vineyards that I am delighted to live next to. The sheep are "working" animals, deployed as natural weed eaters by a local company here called Wooly Weeders. The sheep are trucked in and let loose to dine on the mustard, grass, and other consumables growing in the vineyard. They are chaperoned by Border collies who maneuver the flock and two Great Pyrenees who ward off coyotes, mountain lions, and bears—and, in our vineyards, jackrabbits, squirrels, hawks, and owls.

The Great Pyrenees are friendly giants who wag their tails as neighborhood dogs make their way with their owners down our "Doggy Path," but who also bark instructions letting the gawkers (pet owners) and pets know that work is being done and not to get too close or interfere. I have a ringside seat and watch through my kitchen window.

Gratitude

I do lead a charmed life, and I gratefully acknowledge the many blessings that are mine at this moment. I am aware that my preference for my life to always be this way, to stay the same, and to never change, is unrealistic. I try to remember to pay attention and express gratitude for all the bounty. I also am aware that others do not share in these privileges and, instead, experience suffering, fear, and loneliness. I rest in the hope that these experiences will diminish in intensity and frequency, and all beings may be free from suffering.

Some Additional Thoughts

Integrating gratitude into daily activities as we age is beneficial in a number of ways. There are many methods for incorporating gratitude. Keeping a gratitude journal is probably one you are already familiar with. It may not always be easy to find something to be grateful for. In cases like this, I am reminded of Meister Eckhart and his instruction to say "thank you," knowing that will suffice.

CURIOSITY

Originally published October 14, 2018

Alice laughed: "There's no use trying," she said; "one can't believe impossible things." "I daresay you haven't had much practice," said the Queen. "When I was younger, I always did it for half an hour a day. Why, sometimes I've believed as many as six impossible things before breakfast."

–Lewis Carroll, *Through the Looking-Glass*

ONE OF THE MOST IMPORTANT findings in the last few years regarding brain health is that curiosity has benefits. Our brains seem designed to pay attention to novel things, perhaps out of a need to determine threat, but ultimately, apparently, purely out of curiosity. As the Queen observed, however, it is much easier to be curious when we are younger. As we age, there is a tendency for some to fall back on habitual ways of thinking and experiencing.

The benefit of staying curious across the life span is that you get to engage with others. Sometimes others confirm and support your beliefs or ideas. In other cases, others may get your blood boiling because they challenge deeply held beliefs.

Challenging your thinking is like going to the mind gym and lifting weights. It is a much more powerful boost to your brain health than just doing crossword puzzles. And it is so very easy to find challenges to our thinking these days! Just Google any topic, and you can find opinions galore.

Good News/Bad News

Curiosity is more than just wanting to know something. It is also a way we manage anxiety states. For example, many of you have used the Internet to do research on aches, pains, and diagnoses. Why? Because once we find others who have experiences that are similar to ones we have, we feel better. Then again, sometimes we find information that makes us feel worse. Still, asking questions and challenging your thinking seems to be a protective factor in brain health.

Another aspect of curiosity is the degree to which you are open to new experiences (ranging from "not at all" to "whoo-hoo!"). This personality trait is one of the "Big Five" traits shared by all humans:

- Openness to experience
- Conscientiousness
- Extraversion
- Agreeableness
- Neuroticism

Openness to experience is best described as an interest in new and different things. These things can range from trying ethnic food to traveling to exotic locations. Trying new experiences may include doing fun or sometimes scary things just for the thrill of it. It may also include the ability to easily see things from a different perspective and hold a differing point of view without contradiction.

We often see this trait in people who are highly creative, are good problem-solvers, and take risks. If you identify with these adjectives, then you can expect to continue to enjoy the benefits of curiosity. If you don't, however, not to worry. Curiosity can be acquired and comes in amazing ways.

Do What You Love

Finding something you love and doing it on a regular basis seems to light up the same regions of the brain that are lit up in those creative people. So, if you love gardening, you probably look for and seek advice from others who share your passion. You probably hunt through catalogs looking for different plants or vegetables. You probably check out sales at the local garden center. All of these things stimulate your curiosity.

Questions

Asking questions and talking with others are also aspects of curiosity. There are some people who just love asking questions! Hopefully, that skill is balanced with listening to answers. Having a give-and-take dialogue about a shared interest, idea, hobby, or issue sparks different levels of engagement. The more active the engagement, the more benefits for your brain. You can attend a lecture or concert and enjoy yourself. If you talk about it afterward with others and seek out information about the topic or the history of the band, you will get an even bigger bang for your buck.

Your brain literally lights up when it is faced with a problem to solve or a new experience to incorporate. But if the problem you are trying to solve is too difficult or doesn't challenge you enough, your focus will drift away, and the benefit of curiosity will go with it. The greater your ability to pay attention, the greater your benefit from the experience. But if you are feeling afraid, or sad, or tired, the experience itself will be tempered by your feeling unwell. This effect is true for any kind of painful experience. If you have poor or limited concentration because you are in pain all the time, your brain does not have the capacity to be curious for very long.

Template for Curiosity

If you put these ideas all together, you get a template for optimizing curiosity. It looks something like this:

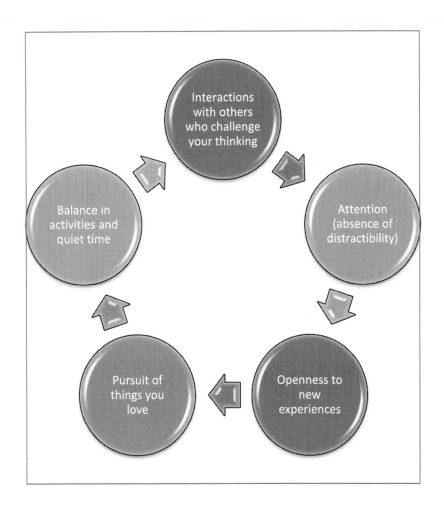

1. Interactions with others who challenge your thinking
2. Openness to new experiences
3. Attention (absence of distractibility)
4. Pursuit of things you love
5. Balance in activities and quiet time

One of the wonderful things about aging is that we have more time to pursue those things that we want to know more about. This activity isn't a luxury! It is an essential strategy for staying cognitively and socially engaged.

A Word of Caution

It is easy today to go online and look things up on Google or Wikipedia or ask Siri or Alexa to handle finding what we want to know. Information is at our fingertips 24/7. The downside is that not all the information we will find is accurate, truthful, or helpful. Many of us need to develop skills in determining fact from fiction. Truly being curious has as its most fundamental basis the willingness to set aside prejudice. Critical thinking skills are essential in sorting through the avalanche of information out there on what is good for you and what is bad.

TAKING THE WATERS

Originally published April 14, 2019

I WAS BACK IN THE POOL today. First time in years. I have rejoined a local swim club that has outdoor lap pools for the hearty and fit, a heated indoor pool for those of us with arthritis, and an expansive hot tub that is outside but heated to a reasonable simmer suitable for soaking tired and achy muscles.

Resistance and Rejoicing

Getting to this goal was a bit of a battle between my body and mind. My mind was in its typical critical space, comparing my body to others and taking inventory of all my deficits. My body, once in the water, rejoiced like a trapped dolphin once freed to move effortlessly through the water. My hips, knees, and ankles, usually numbed by a combination of pressure from the pull of gravity and push of my excess weight, suddenly were out on parole and able to explore a range of motion denied on land.

I was cautious at first. At least my mind was. It let forth a steady stream of coaching tips: "Walk slowly and carefully so you don't slip. Don't get too ambitious. This is your first time back in the water. Say hello to the others in the pool, but don't be too intrusive. Remember to breathe. If it hurts, that is OK, just be gentle."

Relief

My body responded with: "Whoo-hoo! BABY! FREE AT LAST! FREE AT LAST!, THANK GOD ALMIGHTY, I AM FREE AT LAST!" I was mindful that these ecstatic murmurings were under water and not likely to be heard by any of the other swimmers in the pool with me, thereby avoiding the embarrassment of having my exuberance and joy witnessed.

As I looked around the pool, I found myself among more women than men—mostly women who weighed as much as I did and who were as old or older. Much like the monkeys of the hot springs in Nagano, Japan, we were all seeking relief and taking the waters. There was not a lot of conversation, but then again, I was new to the group.

Pool Etiquette

Pool etiquette is interesting, especially for the uninitiated. We are territorial beings. Finding "my" spot in the pool required paying attention to what the others were doing and where. Exercises designed to rehab hips and knees that had undergone replacement surgery were being undertaken by the majority of folks in the pool. There was little aerobic activity.

Conversations were limited to "hello" and "good morning!" All of us were intent on letting the healing properties of the water work magic before we became land mammals once more. We are the modern-day legatees of those ancients who found healing in hot springs, attended community baths for cleansing and connecting, and noticed the benefits of water in rejuvenating body, mind, and spirit. Archaeologists and anthropologists have found evidence of humans using waters to heal and cure in every culture. Perhaps this is further evidence of our evolution from water to land.

Water Baby

I have always loved the water. From my earliest days of learning to swim at the Nineteenth Century Women's Club pool, where I couldn't touch the bottom and was scared to go into the deep end, to skinny-dipping at night in glorious Lake George in upstate New York, I have found excitement, joy, exercise, strength, endurance, and delight. At one time I was a water safety instructor for the American Red Cross. I met my husband through water activities, and we shared a love of swimming and all kinds of water-related recreation. I learned to meditate by swimming laps late at night in a pool lit only with underwater lights.

Returning to this familiar environment was a bit of a shock, though. My limbs have lost their strength and flexibility; my lungs no longer push the air out forcefully, stroke after stroke. What I am admitting here is that I am seriously out of shape. But the water doesn't care. It holds the promise of getting me back to healthy and pain-free movement. As long as I show up, it will provide buoyancy, resistance, and challenge. As long as I quiet my mind and remember that my body delights in playing in this blissful environment, I will grow in strength, stamina, and flexibility.

Water Exercise Rocks!

I am both amazed and delighted that so many older adults are finding their way into pools across the country. All forms of movement can be found in YMCA pools, private clubs, and wellness programs offered by hospitals. Water aerobics, water yoga, water exercise, water massage, and water rehabilitation are among preferred forms of exercise for many aging adults. I recently read an article by a physical therapist encouraging people needing to have hip and knee replacement surgery to start doing "pre-hab" in the water *before* the surgery to optimize muscles and tendons and get the body ready for the new parts that will replace the old, worn-out joints.

I also know I am in the midst of my exercise honeymoon. I do not yet require United Nations negotiating teams to get me out of bed and into the pool. I am committed to restoring myself for now. And there will come a time when the seduction of staying in bed may override the disciplined me, and I might slip back into bad habits. By writing this, however, I am committing to changing for the better and establishing a routine that will keep me healthy now and into my elderhood.

It's Not All in Your Mind

Sometimes the barriers to getting up and moving around aren't desire or intention. Maybe you don't have a safe place to exercise, or extra money to join a gym or pool. These are legitimate issues. Finding ways to exercise in your own home requires being creative, but it can be done. Singing and dancing all by yourself in the comfort of your "home" are also wonderful ways to keep your body and soul moving.

If it's been a while since you moved at all, then start slowly and build up gradually. Set small goals so that you feel good about accomplishing them. Seek information online or from physical therapists for possible routines. Starting something is hard, I will admit. Keeping up an exercise program can seem daunting. So don't think about it that way. Change your thoughts and change your behavior. Then just keep coming back to what works for you and do a little bit more.

MOAB

Originally published October 27, 2019

THIS PAST WEEK I TRAVELED to a spot on our planet that I had never visited before. I joined a dear friend in Moab, Utah. I have written before about how taking a trip shifts my consciousness and reboots my emotional self. This trip was no different. What *was* different has everything to do with the "where" of this trip. The "who" and the "how" also played roles, but the true transformation came about because of the "where."

I remember taking my first journalism writing class, where I was taught the "five Ws": who, what, where, when, and how. This structural format lends itself to succinct column inches for the author and predictable reading for the reader. The older I get, the more I appreciate this kind of intrinsic structure and the more I seem to benefit when I am able to tap into it. In trying to capture the impact of this trip, I am finding the five W's are very useful.

Who

My fellow traveler was a college classmate with whom I have a shared history of forty-eight years. This binds both of us to a time when we were exploring who we were becoming, lo, those many decades ago, all the way to the wise, productive, and engaged women we have become. This is a very enriching and supportive friendship that I value.

We are now both what is termed the "young-old" (between the ages of sixty-five and seventy-four). The definition of this term is both confusing and misleading because it relies solely on chronology. My friend and I both agreed that we may look "older" on the outside, but we feel and act much younger than our chronological years in spite of arthritis, chronic health conditions, and (for me) a new hip.

What

The "doing" of this trip consisted of driving through some extraordinarily beautiful country, eating at roadside spots, deciding what sightseeing was worthy of our time, grabbing local food at restaurants and grocery stores, purchasing trinkets and memorabilia, spending time reminiscing, and watching local TV. All of which resulted in some rich encounters with fellow travelers, wildlife, and locals, not to mention allowing us to capture this vast and inspiring land on our smartphones. I needed to road-test my new hip, and this seemed like the perfect opportunity to go for a reasonably short plane ride, spend time in a car, and take short walks putting the hip to the test.

Where

Since my friend lives in upstate New York and was coming to Salt Lake City for business, we decided to meet in SLC and just explore the surrounding area. I had friends who had recently gone to Moab, so I suggested we go take a look and see what we could see. I really had no sense of where this was and didn't appreciate the vastness of the state of Utah until we started the four-hour drive from Salt Lake City.

Utah is one of those western states that has seemingly straight borders but is actually made up of physical features that rise over a mile in the sky in the various mountain ranges, to almost a mile into the ground in the canyon lands and salt flats. When you are on the ground, the vastness of uninterrupted views is breathtaking. When you are in the air, the patterns of roads and towns are remarkably geometric.

When

On the surface, the dates were dictated because of my friend's business obligations. Both of us had the flexibility of taking time away from our responsibilities. Turned out that this is also a great time, weather-wise, to be in southeastern Utah; we were in a weather window of relative beneficent temperatures and low precipitation. Our time in Utah brought snow to the elevated peaks of the Wasatch and La Sal Mountains and warm and sunny days to Arches National Park and Canyonlands National Park.

Why

Honestly, we both just needed a break. I needed some respite from recovering after my hip surgery and from what has sadly become known as "fire season" in my northern California home. My friend decided to extend her stay and just enjoy a bit of relaxation after working hard at her conference.

Observations

I am more anxious about getting to the airport than I am about flying. I just hate being late! And I hate having to rely on others to get me where I want to go. I did enjoy the convenience of having airline and airport staff take me by wheelchair from curbside to loading gate. I like having people act kindly toward me since I am using a cane. I tend to milk that kindness.

New places stimulate me in unexpected ways. Somehow my senses are heightened: things taste different (especially water!), things smell different (juniper is my new favorite!), light and shadows invite me to see things in new ways. This trip reminded me how important it is for me to take body lotion. The low humidity and high altitude really dried my skin and lips out.

I have lots of judgments about people who travel. I am particularly irked by folks who are speaking loudly while on their cell phones and don't seem to be aware that they are actually shouting. I am also irked by folks who leave their garbage behind instead of putting it in the bins provided. I am also incredibly curious about these people. I wonder what their hopes and dreams are and whether they are happy or experiencing challenges. Salt Lake City is home to happy Mormons. There is a very different feel to this airport than the one in San Francisco.

Coming home is always enjoyable. I experience familiar landmarks with changed eyes, seeing them in a new way that is comforting. Coming home to my own shower and bed is always a joy.

Takeaways

This trip challenged me to use my new hip and put it to the test. The hip did really well. I need some encouragement to trust more and challenge myself to do more.

I was brought to tears on more than one occasion when I realized the following: I am truly insignificant in the vastness of time and universal change, yet I am an intrinsic part of that vastness and change. This insight into the gift of belonging while being impermanent gave me relief from the self-imposed gerbil wheel of work and achievement I find myself mindlessly engaged with.

I understood, in I way I have never grasped before, the depth and meaning of the Navajo Way Blessing Ceremony:

Walking in Beauty:
Closing Prayer from the Navajo Way Blessing Ceremony

In beauty I walk
With beauty before me I walk
With beauty behind me I walk
With beauty above me I walk
With beauty around me I walk
It has become beauty again
Hózhóogo naasháa doo
Shitsijí' hózhóogo naasháa doo
Shikéédéé hózhóogo naasháa doo
Shideigi hózhóogo naasháa doo
T'áá altso shinaagóó hózhóogo naasháa doo
Hózhó náhásdlíí' Hózhó náhásdlíí'
Hózhó náhásdlíí' Hózhó náhásdlíí'
Today I will walk out, today everything negative will leave me.
I will be as I was before, I will have a cool breeze over my body.
I will have a light body, I will be happy forever, nothing will hinder me.
I walk with beauty before me.
I walk with beauty behind me.
I walk with beauty below me.
I walk with beauty above me.

I walk with beauty around me.
My words will be beautiful.
In beauty all day long may I walk.
Through the returning seasons, may I walk.
On the trail marked with pollen may I walk.
With dew about my feet, may I walk.
With beauty before me may I walk.
With beauty behind me may I walk.
With beauty below me may I walk.
With beauty above me may I walk.
With beauty all around me may I walk.
In old age wandering on a trail of beauty, lively, may I walk.
In old age wandering on a trail of beauty, living again, may I walk.
My words will be beautiful . . .

I am already planning my next trip!

SABBATICAL

Originally published February 16, 2020

I AM GETTING READY TO go on a month-long trip. This will be the longest I have been away from my practice in more than twenty years. It is also the longest I have been away from home since I was in college and spent what we called January Independent Study Term (JIST) enjoying a break from the classroom and joining our professors in studying or traveling somewhere with the sole purpose of experiential learning.

Soul Purpose

Truth be told, "sole purpose" can easily be replaced with "soul purpose," since the term "sabbatical" arises from a Hebrew word "shabbat" (day of rest) and instructions from Leviticus to undertake a break every seven years (*shmita*). I intend to use this time away to slow down, recalibrate my body clock, and find a new pace that I will be able to sustain over the coming decades.

In looking back over the past ten years, I am amazed at how much of my life has been focused on health issues, managing my practice, starting new ventures, and learning to live my life as a widow. After my husband died, I had to manage financial challenges as well as emotional ones. I was blessed to have friends who gave me unconditional support and work that paid well and provided benefits. The price I paid, however, was to run my body into the ground. I have been in pain for the past seven years. Only now, after having had both my hips replaced, do I fully appreciate the degree of functional impairment I was dealing with.

In spite of the physical challenges, I remained in the classroom, kept up a private practice, wrote a book, and lectured to groups of therapists across the country. All these things gave me great pleasure and incredible opportunities to grow, but I was also tired, overweight, depressed, and in need of much better self-care. I did take a trip in 2013 with a dear friend to the Mediterranean. We started in Rome and ended up in Barcelona. I realized then how much I missed traveling.

Seven Year Itch

It is now 2020. If my math is correct, it's been seven years! I seriously doubt that I have a subliminal Levite calendar that notifies me when I need to take time away from tending the fields, but it is an interesting coincidence that in the past year or so I have somehow organized my life so that I have the means, the opportunity, and the physical health to take time away from my practice and do some soul-searching.

Heading Down Under

I am traveling to New Zealand. This is one of my bucket list destinations. When I was quite a young child, I read *Erewhon* by Samuel Butler. Turns out Butler actually spent several years in New Zealand, and much of the book was inspired by his time there. At the time, I did not appreciate the work as the satire Butler intended; rather, I fell in love with the descriptions of the country and have wanted to travel to New Zealand ever since.

Over the decades I have toyed with the idea of moving to New Zealand. My husband and I spent hours going over possible emigration scenarios. Today it seems to be closer to the Utopian ideal that Butler described and offers much that agrees with my way of thinking about living close with nature, managing the environment, and sustainability, not to mention jaw-dropping vistas as well as placid sheep. Rumor has it they also grow a rather fine sauvignon wine grape there.

The trip itself actually came about while I was watching TV and caught an ad for a cruise to Alaska. This is another of my bucket list destinations. I called a friend who books cruises to see whether she could arrange the trip. Instead, I got a call back saying, "How would you like to cruise to New Zealand?" That started the ball rolling. I looked at my calendar, decided that I also needed a couple of days in Hawaii as well as at least a week in Sydney, Australia, so I just went ahead and booked it.

When the Moon Is in the Seventh House

This all may sound impulsive, but it really is not. What happened was just that the stars aligned with my desires and I let go of all the "shoulds" that have kept me from making this trip in the past. I also followed the wise words of several of my close friends, all of whom are intrepid travelers and who swear by travel as a way to stay engaged with life, learn new things, meet different people, and generally keep their brain cells firing at optimum levels.

I know many folks who have experienced modern-day travel as challenging. I used to have that attitude also, but because of the two years I spent flying around the United States lecturing, I learned a couple of tricks to better manage my frustrations. First and foremost, get to the airport early. Make sure you have TSA PreCheck so you don't have to take your shoes off or wait in long lines. If you can, just take a carry-on. That way you don't have to wait to pick up your luggage at the other end. Finally, take something good to read and a battery charger. You will inevitably have to wait, so don't sweat it!

I Get to Fly!

While these strategies have been useful, what was the most helpful, inspiring, and—pardon the pun—uplifting, was something my traveling companion to the Mediterranean said to me. She is a seventy-something former Pan Am stewardess ("flight attendant" nowadays), who flies almost weekly around the United States and goes overseas when she can.

She called me up before going on a trip and said, "I get to fly!" with such joy in her voice that I had to ask what she meant by that. I was used to the grousing, complaining, and generally negative attitude to air travel adopted by so many. But she reminded me of the awe that flying really inspires: it is an engineering marvel that allows us to break the bonds of gravity and see the clouds from above, overcome the obstacles of time and distance, and be transported to a different spot on the earth, all within the comfort of a pressure -and temperature-controlled conveyance that arrives safely and on time (mostly) and is flown by some very handsome pilots to boot (I will own that sexist comment—I am a sucker for a pilot!).

JUBILATION

Originally published November 8, 2020

This was written just after Joseph A. Biden was elected president.

DON'T GET ME WRONG. I am over the moon with happiness at the outcome of this election. It does feel good to be a "winner." I am so relieved I no longer have to listen to the talking heads parse endless scenarios of doom. And I will slowly permit myself the luxury of imagining a hopeful future. I am going to take the time and enjoy this sweet moment of crossing a finish line that seemed to always be just out of reach. But what price do we pay for winning?

There will be a chorus of "let the healing begin!"—which is catchy and does need to be sung—and yet there are still wounds that need to be debrided. Over these last few years, I have found that my beliefs and understanding about people I have shared my life with have often been wrong. My comfort zone with hypocrisy is nonexistent. My expectations of how "good" people should act rely more now on social media memes and late-night comedians' monologues than what is told to me from the pulpit or taught in a classroom.

Council of Elders

If this were another time and another culture, I would expect a council of elders to meet, consider what would be best for the whole, and announce their plans at a gathering. Instead, I suspect each side will fall in behind their spokes-channels and be fed a script that will be parroted over and over again on Twitter, Facebook, Instagram, TikTok and WhatsApp.

Should I be invited to the council, I would offer the following as points to ponder in the coming days:

How did we get to this place where half of us see the world one way and half see it another?
How did we come to decide that it is no longer in our best interest to collaborate and cooperate?

How do we overcome the built-up resentment and mistrust that now occupy our energies?

How many ways forward are there that don't require us to believe the same things before we can figure out how to put out the fire that is burning our house down?

What can we do to increase our capacity for not knowing and decrease our need for being right all the time?

How can I learn to see the "other" in you and not be threatened by that?

Who or what can show us a way we can we admit that there are some things that we can't do all by ourselves and that in joining together, things can be accomplished that would surely fail otherwise?

How can we give each other a time-out to lick our wounds, absorb all the change that has gone on over the past four years, and not keep adding to the inventory of insult and accusation?

What sources of wisdom can we tap into that will engender hope?

What resources are there that we can share and still have enough for ourselves?

What do I have to accept to move forward?

What do I have to hold on to in order to move forward?

What am I willing to let go of in order to move forward?

When will I be ready?

I don't have answers to these questions. But I do have time and space to explore them with you and with others. I invite you to answer these questions. Spend some time reflecting on what you are feeling today. How can you use that experience to heal?

Victory or Defeat?

Yes, I am feeling jubilation. But just for a brief moment. I realize that there are others who are in mourning. Theirs was not the joyful victory; rather it was a bittersweet defeat. Their feelings are as intense as mine, but with a different consequence. While I am feeling relief, they are experiencing betrayal. While I am feeling validation, they are feeling scorn. It was only four years ago that I experienced these feelings, too. When my candidate lost, I felt disconnected, abandoned, and without hope. My lesson in that experience is serving me well at this juncture.

My lesson is this: things change. Not always the way I want them to. Not always on my timeline. I can be overwhelmed with joy or disappointment and still find a way to do the things I need to do. I can be bitter or generous, and experience the consequences of those choices. I can be emboldened to speak my truth and learn that some people are offended by it while others may embrace me. The challenge here is understanding that the universe cares little for my preferences, yet I am responsible for the impact my words and actions have on those who are known to me as well as those who are unknown.

Uncomfortable Discoveries

The greatest toll of these past four years has been on my sense of community and belonging. I am saddened to learn how many of my family members and friends harbor hatred and prejudice. I am ashamed that my silence has been taken as tacit acceptance of racism and that it took me this long to get that. I am inspired to seek opportunities to create community in new and more inclusive ways. This experience has acted as a mirror reflecting my own ways of being in the world, and I am wanting to change what I see.

There is much to be healed and much work to be done.

ABOUT THE AUTHOR

MARY L. FLETT, PHD is an author who used to be a psychologist. In addition to writing, she is a nationally-recognized speaker and has led seminars on aging across the country. In this second book in her series, *Aging with Finesse*, she shares her insights and wisdom gleaned from over 30 years of working with elders as a psychologist, and a lifetime of mentoring by older friends and relatives. She is the Executive Director of the Center for Aging and Values and, in her spare time, runs Five Pillars of Aging, offering online and in-person programs on how to age better and age well.

Made in the USA
Columbia, SC
07 December 2021

50634438R00089